TREASURE OF QUMRAN

TREASURE OF QUMRAN

My Story of the Dead Sea Scrolls

ATHANASIUS YESHUE SAMUEL

THE WESTMINSTER PRESS
Philadelphia

FRONTISPIECE:
*The author, His Excellency Archbishop Athanasius
Yeshue Samuel, holding the famed Isaiah Scroll
during its premiere exhibition at the Library of
Congress in Washington, D.C., in October, 1949
Photo courtesy of Harris & Ewing News Service*

Published by The Westminster Press ®
Philadelphia, Pennsylvania

PRINTED IN THE UNITED STATES OF AMERICA

To my Mother, Khatoun

Who has guided my life's voyage from a simple cabin in Mesopotamia to an archbishop's head-quarters in the United States of America; whose keenness of memory has illuminated many shadows in the recollections of my early years; and whom God in his goodness has vouchsafed to preserve to me until this very day,

This book, with love and gratitude,

is

dedicated

CONTENTS

FOREWORD

Here is a moving autobiography of the man who purchased the first of the Dead Sea Scrolls which were found by the Ta'amireh Bedouins in the Judean Wilderness, northwest of the Dead Sea. He tells his whole life from birth down to the present. Most importantly, he relates how he obtained these most ancient Jewish manuscripts, including a copy of The Book of Isaiah a thousand years older than any previously known copy in Hebrew.

He was a poor farm boy fleeing for his life from Turkish persecutors of the Syrian Christians during World War I, and he was left sick and exhausted by a Syrian roadside to die. Yet the hand of Providence spared his life and provided for his education and spiritual training, until in 1946 he became the Metropolitan (or Archbishop) of the Syrian Orthodox Archdiocese of Jerusalem. The following year he bought the first four Dead Sea Scrolls that were discovered, and seven months later he made them available for study and publication by the American School of Oriental Research in Jerusalem. Meanwhile, despite many discouragements, he had maintained his faith in the antiquity of the scrolls and in their probable Essene origin, in view of their discovery in a cave near the Dead Sea.

In previous years he had received the best education his church had to offer and had become an expert on the history and theology of his own church, whose literature dates back to the early centuries of the Christian era. He became a student of old documents in Syriac, so he knew the materials of manuscripts and the marks of antiquity. He was also well versed in ancient Jewish history and so knew of the ancient Essenes who had once resided in the wilderness west of the Dead Sea. His studies at the St. Mark's Monastery in Jerusalem were rounded out by a year in the Coptic Theological College in Cairo, Egypt, and by travels throughout the Middle East. Thus he was well prepared for his part in the exciting drama of the discovery of the Dead Sea Scrolls.

In early 1949, he came to the United States, bringing with him his four ancient documents, which he later sold and which are now in Jerusalem, Israel, where they are kept with other manuscripts from the same cave which had been purchased from the Arabs by the late Prof. E. L. Sukenik, of Hebrew University. His Eminence, the Most Reverend Samuel, has become an American citizen, and he is today the Metropolitan of the Syrian Orthodox Archdiocese of the United States and Canada, with headquarters in Hackensack, New Jersey. He is the first Syrian Archbishop to reside in the United States.

As one of the American scholars who participated in the first study of these ancient manuscripts, I have been asked by His Grace, the Metropolitan, to write this foreword and to discuss the character and significance of these old manuscripts which he still treasures so highly.

A PHENOMENAL DISCOVERY

"My heartiest congratulations on the greatest manuscript discovery of modern times!"

So wrote William F. Albright to the American School of Oriental Research at Jerusalem, in a letter received March 15, 1948. Dr. John C. Trever, a Fellow at the school, had sent him photographs of two columns of the complete Isaiah Scroll which we had photographed on February 21. On the basis of the style of penmanship, Dr. Albright, a noted Orientalist and archaeologist at Johns Hopkins University, had concluded:

> "There is no doubt in my mind that the script
> is more archaic than that of the Nash Papyrus.
> ... I should prefer a date around 100 B.C. ...
> What an incredible find! And there can happily
> not be the slightest doubt in the world about
> the genuineness of the manuscript."

Dr. John C. Trever and I, who were Fellows at the school, had already reached similar conclusions based on paleography, the science of dating by penmanship. There were other marks of antiquity as well. Even before that, but unknown to us, Dr. E. L. Sukenik, of Hebrew University, had obtained other manuscripts from the same find and had been shown at least part of these manuscripts also, and had dated them paleographically to the period of the Second Temple, that is, to a time before the Romans destroyed Jerusalem in A.D. 70. He had not informed the Syrians exactly how ancient they were, however. It was in order to learn more about the documents, therefore, that they brought them to the American School of Oriental Research.

The scrolls that Dr. Sukenik obtained were a fragmentary copy of Isaiah, a scroll of sectarian hymns, and a document that he dubbed "The War of the Sons of Light with the Sons of Darkness." All these were in Hebrew. The manuscripts that we examined at the American School were a complete copy of Isaiah, a commentary upon Habakkuk, a manual of discipline giving the regulations and beliefs of an ancient Jewish sect, and an apocryphal rewriting of Genesis. The first three manuscripts brought to the American School were in Hebrew and were remarkably well preserved; but the fourth was in Aramaic and was so brittle and badly stuck together that it could not be opened. It was only after this group of manuscripts were brought to America by the Syrian Archbishop Athanasius Samuel, and then sold to a New York industrialist who turned them over to Israel, that the fourth scroll was opened sufficiently to establish the real nature of its text. Even today, it has not been completely opened. The difficulty with this manuscript is that it was interlined with a blank scroll with which it was rolled. The blank scroll adhered to the written surface of the underlying manuscript. The problem is one of removing the former without ripping off the ink of the inscribed manuscript. The text that has so far been obtained has major characters of Genesis retell their own story in the first person. The narrative is very interesting and gives us our first extensive manuscript in Aramaic from a period roughly contemporary with Christ.

Since the initial find, the manuscript cave has been rediscovered and excavated (February, 1949). It yielded fragments of seventy other rolls. Fragments of the jars in which the scrolls had been stored and pieces of linen cloth in which they had been wrapped were discovered. The linen was subjected to a radiocarbon test to determine the year the flax was grown, and the date A.D. 30 was obtained. Although the scientists at that time did not claim that this method of dating was closer than 90 percent correct, subsequent excavations indicate that the deposit of the scrolls in the cave was probably A.D. 68. Since not all, if any, of these linen wrappers would be new cloth, this particular radiocarbon test was virtually 100 percent correct.

Other manuscript-producing caves near the first have been found. In the fourth there were fragments of over four hundred manuscripts. The eleventh cave contained a scroll of Leviticus, an Aramaic translation of Job, three psalm scrolls, a document called the New Jerusalem Scroll, an apocryphal work based upon the book of Leviticus, and numerous other compositions.

The first scrolls were found in the vicinity of an ancient Jewish religious center, known in Arabic as Khirbet Qumran. The site has been excavated over a period of years (1951–1956) by the archaeologist of Jordan, under the direction of Dr. Roland de Vaux, a Dominican priest and Director of the École Biblique et Archéologique Française in Jerusalem. As early as the spring of 1948, the Metropolitan referred to Qumran in his conversations (but not by name) as near the manuscript caves. He wondered whether it

and the adjoining cemetery could be that of the ancient
Essenes, for according to him no one had resided in this
area since these Jews who were there in the time of Christ.
The excavations showed that this was the community center
of a Jewish sect which was first settled about 125 to 100 B.C.
and was destroyed by an earthquake about 31 B.C. It was
rebuilt about the turn of the Christian era and served the
same purpose until it was destroyed in A.D. 68 by Vespasian,
whose troops reused and adapted a portion of the site as
a military fort. Everything found suited the known character of the ancient Essenes, a monastic (or semimonastic)
sect of Jews who had an important settlement west of the
Dead Sea. The pottery was from the same period and of
the same type as that found in the nearby caves, including
the first cave in which alone the manuscripts had been
deposited in jars. Meanwhile, I had already translated The
Manual of Discipline and had shown the Essene affinities
of the sect. The earliest convictions of the Syrian Metropolitan had been vindicated.

These discoveries near Khirbet Qumran are frequently
called the Qumran Scrolls in order to distinguish them from
other unrelated discoveries in the desert west of the Dead
Sea. Among them are manuscripts left in caves farther south
by officers and soldiers of Simon ben Kosibah (better known
as Bar Kokhba), who led a revolt against Rome, in A.D. 132–
135. Some of these finds were made in caves in Jordan,
others in Israel. Manuscripts found in the ruins of an ancient Greek Orthodox monastery, known today as Khirbet
Mird, included classical texts in Greek and Latin, also
manuscripts of the New Testament in Palestinian Syriac,
dating from the sixth to the eighth centuries A.D. The place
of this discovery is only a few miles northwest of Khirbet
Qumran, inside Jordan. A few miles north of Jericho, and
therefore outside the area generally included in the Judean
Wilderness, legal and commercial papyruses were found
in 1962. These had been taken to a cave by fugitives from
Samaria in 331 B.C., which was then under attack by Alexander the Great. In the excavations of the ancient fortress

of Masada, in the Israeli part of the Judean Wilderness, in 1961 and 1962, the vestiges of scrolls were found, including Gen. 46:7-11; Lev. 4:3-9; Ps. 81:3 to 85:10, and an apocryphal document giving the Songs of the Sabbath Sacrifice. Thus the discoveries in this area of the Holy Land are continuing; and the Metropolitan Samuel's scrolls were but the beginning of a whole series of important finds.

Since the wilderness has produced so much in recent years, one may ask why finds were not made here earlier. One explanation is that archaeologists had been more concerned with the excavation of cities in the damper and more populous areas of the country than in exploring desert caves. However, a study of ancient history has revealed that some discoveries were made in this desert in ancient times. Most Biblical scholars were unaware of this; but some of the evidence for this was known to Metropolitan Samuel who had become acquainted with the texts of the church fathers in his studies at the St. Mark's Monastery. From the story of his life, one can see that this was one of the facts which inspired his undiscourageable conviction that these scrolls were both genuine and very old.

One of these ancient finds was referred to in a marginal note in Origen's Hexapla, according to which the sixth column of his parallel texts of the psalms was derived from a manuscript found in company with other Greek and Hebrew books in a jar near Jericho during the reign of Antoninus, son of Severus (A.D. 211–217). There was also, according to Rabbinic sources, a Jericho copy of the Pentateuch that was used by the Masoretes in helping establish the traditional text of the Bible. Whether this was a part of the same or another discovery is unknown.

Most importantly there is the account of Timotheus I, Patriarch of Seleucia (A.D. 726–819), in a Syriac letter to Sergius, Metropolitan of Elam (who died about A.D. 805). According to a story reported to the Patriarch by a Jewish convert to his church, some books had been recently found in a cave near Jericho. The catechumen reported: "We have found more than 200 Psalms of David among our books."

At the time of the Patriarch's writing, this had happened some ten years earlier. Despite his efforts to confirm the discoveries, he had learned nothing; but the whole matter was still according to him "a fire in my heart, burning and blazing in my bones." He therefore urged the Metropolitan of Elam to do all in his power to find these scrolls and to translate them. There is no good reason to doubt that an important Dead Sea Scroll discovery was made about A.D. 795 or earlier, for traditions concerning this discovery have been preserved also in Jewish sources, both Rabbinic and Qaraite.

In 1895, Dr. Solomon Schechter, who later became the president of the Jewish Theological Seminary in New York, discovered in a sealed-off storage room (or genizah) of a medieval synagogue in Old Cairo a large number of manuscripts, including texts of the Qaraite Jewish sect. Among them were large portions of two manuscripts of two different recensions of a previously unknown work that he dubbed the "Zadokite Work," also portions of the Hebrew text of Ecclesiasticus, or the Wisdom of Jesus the Son of Sirach, which had been known only in translation before. Scholars disputed the antiquity of these texts, since the manuscripts that contained them were themselves medieval. Yet Solomon Schechter believed that they were descended from pre-Christian prototypes. Portions of the so-called Zadokite Work have turned up in the fourth and sixth Qumran caves. Two small fragments of the Hebrew of Ecclesiasticus were found in the second Qumran cave, and much larger portions have been found in Masada, which was destroyed by the Romans in A.D. 73. The Hebrew in each case agrees sufficiently to prove textual descent, so that the view that the Hebrew text of the Cairo Genizah was simply a medieval translation made into Hebrew from the Greek has been proved false. In the wake of these discoveries, it has been suggested that these Cairo manuscripts had been copied from Dead Sea Scrolls which were found in the eighth century A.D. It is even argued that many of the distinctive beliefs of the Qaraites were

based on such manuscripts. Here is the answer to those
who at first questioned the authenticity of the sectarian
texts of Qumran on the ground of their affinity with certain
texts of the Qaraites.

Roughly one third of the Qumran texts are Biblical. They
are copies, mostly incomplete and fragmentary, of Old
Testament books. From the fourth cave alone there are
fragments of every book of the Old Testament, unless it
be Esther. Several copies of some of the books are represented, particularly Deuteronomy, Isaiah, the Minor
Prophets, and The Psalms—which seem to be the most
popular works of the Jewish sect that copied these manuscripts. Prior to the discovery of the Dead Sea Scrolls, our
most ancient texts in Hebrew were mostly from the eighth
to the tenth centuries A.D. With the new discovery we are
thrown back with a bound a whole thousand years. We did
have the assistance hitherto of ancient versions. A version
is a translation from the original tongue into some other
language. Thus the Septuagint is a Greek translation prepared in Alexandria, Egypt, during the last three centuries
B.C. Later versions include other Greek, Syriac, Latin,
and Ethiopic translations. These were made from Hebrew
manuscripts older than those available to us until the discovery of the Qumran Scrolls. These ancient versions have
been an important source for correcting our Hebrew text
of the Old Testament. The newly found manuscripts often
contain the readings of the ancient versions and even many
of the readings that were pure guesses before. They have
thereby vindicated the work of Old Testament textual
criticism.

Mostly, however, the Biblical texts offer us new tools
for textual criticism. It is no easy matter to use these tools,
for some of the manuscripts contain scribal errors of their
own. In the complete Isaiah Scroll, the text has been subtly
altered at times in order to bring out sectarian interpreta-
tions. Besides all this, there are different text types of some
of the books. In the case of the Pentateuch, the first five
books of the Bible, there are three different text types.

One of these is very similar to the traditional Hebrew text used in translating our Bibles. Another is very much like the Septuagint that was translated in the third century B.C. There are even some manuscripts which are closely related to the Samaritan Pentateuch; but there are no readings reported supporting Samaritan doctrines. Three scrolls of the books of Samuel from the fourth cave are very close to the Septuagint where it departs from the traditional Hebrew text. Yet portions of other Samuel scrolls attest the existence of manuscripts agreeing with the books of Samuel in our Bible. One fragment of Jeremiah contains a passage whose verses are in the order of the Septuagint rather than that of our Bibles. It also omits certain materials that are omitted by the Septuagint.

What these manuscripts do is to take us back to the time when various recensions of the Old Testament books existed side by side. To understand this, we need only to note modern publication practices. An author publishes a book and later gets out a revised and enlarged edition. In the case of textbooks, a revision may be made after the original author has died. Biblical books went through similar revisions. One of the most striking aspects of the Dead Sea Scroll discoveries is the proof that the traditional Hebrew text on which the King James Version was based already existed in substantially its present form in the time of Christ. However, other text types also existed at that time, and sometimes these other text types are more likely original. That is particularly true in the case of I and II Samuel.

The most interesting departures from our Bible are to be seen in a psalm scroll from the eleventh Qumran cave, which has just been published. It contains most of Psalms 101 to 150, but they are arranged in a different order. Many of the individual psalms read very much as in our Bibles, but a few differ considerably. This scroll contains seven additional psalms not found in the Bible and a prose composition describing David's religious and literary genius. It lists the number of different types of psalms that David was supposed to have composed, to a total of 4,050. Two of these psalms correspond to Psalm 151 of the Septuagint, but they are in an entirely different recension. Two others were known previously in a few medieval Syriac manuscripts, which contained two additional psalms not yet attested elsewhere. Another Qumran psalm was previously known in a radically revised and toned-down edition found at the end of the apocryphal book of Ecclesiasticus. The rest were not known at all.

It could be that all four of the extra Syriac psalms (not counting Psalm 151, which appears also in the Septuagint) were derived from the medieval scroll discovery mentioned above. Perhaps there was found a psalm scroll like that of the eleventh Qumran cave, only more complete, and containing therefore all four, instead of only two, of these Syriac psalms. It is also possible that these other psalms appeared in another sectarian document, for hymns are to be found in many of the Qumran manuscripts, and the greatest work of this kind is the Scroll of Thanksgiving Hymns. Although none of these Essene works have survived in the Cairo Genizah or elsewhere, their possible presence in the eighth-century discovery could explain the report that over two hundred psalms of David had been found. Their attribution to David could be due to a statement in the 11Q Psalm Scroll to the effect that David had composed a total of 4,050. An uncritical scholar might be led by this to count every hymn he could find in the total manuscript discovery. If this suggestion is true, the urgent request of the Patriarch Timotheus to the Metropolitan of Damascus to seek out previously unknown Hebrew texts and to translate them may not have been without some fruit.

The people of the scrolls were Jews living on the threshold of the Messianic age, and the two thirds of the scrolls that are non-Biblical reflect their own distinctive beliefs. It is impossible to discuss many of these here, but they are enormously important for helping scholars determine the Semitic backgrounds of primitive Christianity. Prior to

this discovery, there was a strong tendency to underesti-
mate the Palestinian, Jewish background of the New
Testament. How many of the Apocrypha and Pseudepi-
grapha of the Old Testament were based upon Semitic
originals was in dispute. It was generally supposed that
the most important Jewish sources must have been composed in Greek, although the existence of some Palestinian
Aramaic literature was not excluded. The late Edgar Good-
speed went so far as to deny that Hebrew and Aramaic
were employed as literary languages at all at the time the
New Testament was written. The surprising result of all
the recent manuscript discoveries is the demonstration
that Hebrew was far from being a dead language. Not only
is fully 95 percent of the literature of Qumran in Hebrew,
but legal documents and military correspondence were
sometimes written in Hebrew as late as the second century
A.D. as shown by the finds in the Bar Kokhba caves. Only
an occasional scrap of Greek has been found, apart from
extensive remains of a special Greek recension of the
Twelve Minor Prophets. Aramaic, which was most com-
monly employed in oral communication, did indeed receive a minor place compared with Hebrew. Yet some important works were composed in Aramaic.

Among the Aramaic texts are the Genesis Apocryphon
described above, a targum, or translation, of Leviticus, a
targum of Job, several copies of a manuscript describing
the New Jerusalem (including the arrangement of streets
and the architecture and finishings of the houses!). There
are eight partly preserved manuscripts of Enoch, all in
Aramaic, which correspond with various degrees of agreement with four of the five major sections of that work,
which in the English translation of R. H. Charles, consists
of 108 chapters. The second section of Enoch (the Simili-
tudes referring to the heavenly Son of Man) is unfortunately
lacking among these finds. Perhaps this shows that this
section had its literary origin in a different milieu from
that of Qumran. The book of Tobit is represented by three
fragments, one in Hebrew, the other two in Aramaic. There

are also fragments of the Testament of Levi in Aramaic.

Probably the greatest surprise among the discoveries was the Prayer of Nabonidus in Aramaic. Nabonidus was the father of Belshazzar, who was coregent with his father in the last days of the Neo-Babylonian Empire. Since Nabonidus is not mentioned in Daniel, it was supposed that the Jews had entirely forgotten about him; but it now appears that though the Palestinian compiler of the stories in Daniel left him out of account, some Jews never forgot him, and so the Prayer of Nabonidus came to be included among the documents of Qumran.

There has recently been published what is alleged to be a portion of a horoscope concerning a Messianic figure who was expected at Qumran. Like Esau and David, he is to have red hair (Gen. 25:25; I Sam. 16:12; 17:42); like Jacob, he is to feast on red lentils (Gen. 25:34).

Although he will be ignorant in his youth, he will acquire wisdom when he learns the secret knowledge of three books. After that his fame for wisdom will go out to all the world (reminding one of Solomon), and he will exercise the Messianic authority described in the prophecy of Isaiah (ch. 11:1-4). "He will know the secrets of all living beings; and all plots against him will come to an end. His dominion over all living will be very great. His own [p]lans [will succeed (?)], because the chosen one of God is His begotten." That there is a reference to God's begotten is declined by one scholar, since the passage reports that he will be in his youth "as a man who does not know knowledge." However, this language of begetting could be that of adoptionism, whereby one who had not previously been God's son (or royal vice-gerent) was appointed by God to that role (Ps. 2:7). Even in the Christian doctrine of the incarnation (which was certainly absent at Qumran), Jesus was born ignorant, but "*increased* in wisdom and in stature, and in favor with God and man." He, too, knew the secrets of men (John 2:25) and was called the "Chosen One" of God (Luke 23:35). According to excellent manuscript authority (followed by *The New English Bible*), John the

Baptist (John 1:34) testified of Jesus: "This is God's Chosen One." In the Gospel, this title probably refers to God's Suffering Servant (Isa. 42:1-4; 49:1-6; 50:4-11; 52:12 to 53:12), for John also hailed him as "the Lamb of God, who takes away the sin of the world" (ch. 1:29).

Thus Aramaic, as well as Hebrew sources, will help us to understand the import of the Gospel; and the Syriac Bible which is in a kindred language may be illumined at some points by the Aramaic literature of Qumran. There may also be some lexical help in the other direction.

It is fitting in the providence of God that a Syrian archbishop played an important role in the discoveries. This should serve as a challenge to some young Syrian Christian to learn Hebrew and become a student of the scrolls themselves. With a thorough knowledge of Syriac, he might make a unique contribution.

WILLIAM H. BROWNLEE

PREFACE

THE AUTOBIOGRAPHY MUST SERVE TWO PURPOSES: IT must record specifically the pertinent facts of the life with which it deals and it must account for the historic processes of the time in which that particular life is lived. Often shyness, fear of reprisal or the bitterness of truth, or simple modesty abort the one while natural limitations—memory's faulty scan, the brief scope of experience—denude the other. Throughout this book I have tried humbly and genuinely to deal with both these aspects but without forgetting that every written work of history or biography or fiction is primarily created for the reader.

In the course of these pages there are facts and incidents. The facts are historic and unquestionable; the incidents, especially in terms of re-created conversations, should be taken as life and literature, for though two purposes are served by the autobiography, two ends must also be met and fact and history need not banish literature and life.

PROLOGUE

The silent telephone seems to have a spirit of its own. It reproaches me with its stillness and demands by its very presence that I pick it up. But I cannot. Not yet.

I pace the floor of my small study. Outside, in the glorious spring afternoon, bright voices of children coming from school dispel the usual quiet of the tree-lined street.

Is this the time? I ask myself. *Is this the way?* I wish I were a boy again myself, free to run and shout and laugh beneath no burden of decision.

Dear God, I pray, *help me to know the right course. For seven years now I have kept the gifts which you entrusted to me. I have sheltered and defended them in the presence of enemies. I have worked with those good men who sought to bring their message to the world. You have honored me by your trust, but my yoke at times, Lord, has been most bitter. I have heard "smuggler," "traitor," "conspirator," shouted against me, and could forbear that but for the slander which perforce touches the office to which I have been raised in your holy service. If this is the time, Lord, and the way, I beg your guidance. I ask your help in the name of Christ, our Savior and our King.*

The sunlight fades now to a softer gold. The children have deserted their games. All would be quiet but for the fingers of yellow fuchsia stirred by some playful breeze to tap upon the window.

To delay is to await another controversy, some unpredicted challenge, some new unfounded scandal. And far off in Jerusalem and Syria, in Iraq, Lebanon, and Jordan, the needs are great: urgently, they require schoolrooms, books, clothing, cash. They cannot expect to be satisfied by a disputed place in scholarly history.

Long distance rings the number for me. He has been expecting my call. "Yes, my friend, I have made my decision. Place an advertisement in the *Wall Street Journal*. Some of the most precious documents in the annals of mankind are about to be sold over the variety counter of a newspaper column."

My friend does not approve of it, but he will oblige me nonetheless.

I replace the telephone. *Dear God*, I pray, *I hope I have done your will.*

Twilight settles softly upon the city of Hackensack in the State of New Jersey in the United States of America, thousands of miles from my native land and my beloved Jerusalem. There is no one with me now to denounce or uphold my decision. But I am a monk; loneliness is no stranger to me.

I sit in an agreeable chair and pack my reliable pipe and I find myself considering at length the twisting, quixotic paths by which I have come to this moment in my life, to this still, spring evening in Hackensack, New Jersey, in the Year of Our Lord, One Thousand Nine Hundred and Fifty-four.

BOOK
ONE

*For we were not and Thou didst create us.
Lost were we and Thou didst find us. Naked
and Thou didst clothe us; and hungry and
Thou didst satisfy us; athirst and Thou didst
give us to drink; we were in poverty and Thou
didst enrich us; strangers and Thou didst
give us to possess Thy Kingdom. Thou didst
grant us to live, O Lord, and Thou didst save
us by Thy mercy.*

—From the Prayer of St. John,
the Golden Mouth, based on the Sixth Psalm

A DECADE INTO OUR TWENTIETH CHRISTIAN CENTURY, it would have been difficult to find upon this spinning globe a more peaceful village than Hilwah. It was a tiny town a few miles south of Nisibin on the ancient rolling plains of Mesopotamia. Syrian Christians professing the faith of the ageless Church of Antioch were the predominant settlers there — simple, honest farmers who had fled the predatory raids of pagan tribesmen in the Kurdistan Mountains of the north. The fingers of history had touched that town and people but softly and a passing traveler would have found the euphoric atmosphere always created by hard work, humility, and happiness.

It was in Hilwah that my parents met and fell in love and in 1906 were united in matrimony. It was here with clay and mortar, brick and board, and his own hands, that my father built his bride two modest rooms, a sheepfold, courtyard, and surrounding wall — in short, their home.

Now, ordinarily, in a neighborly and Christian hamlet such as this, Christmas is the time of reverence and rejoicing. For the men, no work for three whole days; for the women, the joyful duty of preparing the holiday feast — great roasts of mutton, thickly spiced rice pudding, tantalizing raisin-walnut pies. From midnight until Christmas dawn, the entire village will attend divine services in the little church, and while the timeless prayers of chorus, deacons, and celebrants respond to heaven, hundreds of dancing candle flames will be reflected infinitely upon the

golden altar cloths and numerous gilt-edged ikons. But on
Christmas Eve, 1907, Soumay and Khatoun Samuel were
conspicuously absent from their places in the church, and
in their little house all was disorder.

The elaborately beaded costume over which Khatoun
had labored with zeal and patience for so many winter
evenings lay folded on its shelf, and the delicately fash-
ioned wristlets and trinkets of gold and silver intended to
grace her arms graced only the top of a low wooden table
by the doorway.

The night was sharply chilling, but Soumay perspired
as he paced the shadowed courtyard. Inside, his house
cackled with the busyness of old women, and around the
circle of fire by the far wall of the first room an old woman
argued with a wet nurse over the curative powers of herbs
that Soumay had never even heard of.

"But I am the *Da'ye*," the old midwife insisted. "As my
mother was and my daughter shall be. Ours is the knowledge of herbs and remedies. And ours alone." Her voice
trembled with agitation.

The large bosomy woman shifted a small stick with a
straw, raising a spurt of sudden new flame that reddened
her fleshy features. She knew someone, it seemed, who
had once spoken with a real doctor, a learned man from
the great school of the city and he had said . . .

But the old *Da'ye* would not hear it, and her repeated
protests turned Soumay toward the arched entryway of
the bedroom. There another woman stood, and though
she smiled politely, the lazy shake of her shawl-draped
head told Soumay he was still not welcomed there within.

He ran his tongue along his lower lip. His pipe would
be relaxing now, but to smoke would necessitate joining
the two women near the fire, and he was in no mood for
conversation, let alone debate or argument.

He leaned upon the *tannour*, the outdoor oven whose
rounded top was still warm from the afternoon's baking.
Then again he paced his courtyard in the dappled light
of the midwinter moon-swept sky.

It was distressing, this business of being a father, for at the very moment your beloved most needed you, at the utmost height of her pain and glory, no matter how strong and sturdy a husband you were, no matter how well acquainted with hard and tedious work, no matter how independent and healthy the good God had seen fit to make you, there was nothing you could do but circle the courtyard muttering to yourself and listen to the increasing anguished cries, knowing that her gentle hands grasped the woolen folds of her *lehaf* in sacred agony.

From its dark stall across the yard, the ox lowed a rumbled question: Why was his master up and about so early on a workless, winter morning? And it was morning by this time, for far to the north over the craggy Tour-Abdin, the Hermit Mountains, milky dawn threatened the effulgence of the moon, and Soumay realized with a start that silence had fallen within his house. There was no argument or chatter of women, nor could he hear Khatoun's heart-piercing cries or any movement. Only the sputter and snap from the fire. And silence.

"Dear God," he prayed aloud. "Dear God, do not take her from me. Please! Do not take her from me." And he tore into the house and stumbled through the cluster of women around his wife's *lehaf* just in time to see the old *Da'ye* raise up a tiny naked body in one hand and with the other smack it resoundingly on its wrinkled red buttocks. The infant squalled stormily. Soumay fell to his knees beside the wool-soft bed.

Khatoun's small oval of a face was drawn and bloodless. There did not seem to be a breath in her frail body. He leaned over to kiss her forehead and eyelids and joyfully sensed her stirring at his touch. "Is it a son you have now, my husband?" she whispered.

Soumay blushed—in his anxiety for her, he had not noticed. He looked to the circle of faces grinning warmly.

"Yes, my lady. You have given me a son."

A weak smile now lived on her warm lips. Her eyelids flickered, opened fully. She gestured, and the infant, an indignant wailing fury, was given over to her sweet embrace.

"Shall he never stop screaming?" Soumay asked in wonder, but Khatoun smiled and raised the squabbler high above her head. She was pleased. God had done well by her.

"Soumay," she said, "go to the church and tell the priests and our good friends that we have been blessed with a fine, fine son."

He took her hand, and started to rise. "And what is the name of our fine, fine son, my lady?"

She pressed the baby's head against her cheek. "He came to us on Christmas Day, didn't he?"

Happily lightheaded now, Soumay invited all those who had helped to feast on *Kali'ye*, the salted lamb, and thick black coffee, and then he danced about the courtyard and out into the streets of dawn, singing his glorious news.

Khatoun held the baby very close and she whispered him kisses and the centuries-old Syriac name for Jesus. "Yeshue," she whispered, "Little Yeshue." And her tranquillity enveloped the infant like the woolly warmth of her cover. His crying stopped; he snuggled close to her.

There followed then the green and golden days of growing up and except for such incidents that were later retold to me, my memories of that happy time are colorful colloids, mosaics whirling in the kaleidoscope of my heart, not all defined precisely, but each imbued with that first joy and wonder at experiencing God's good world.

My father's image looms stridently across those memories: a tall, strong man with eyes as big and black as olives which in their sudden anger—if I strayed too near the mule's hindquarters or helped a newborn kid escape the pen—could smoke with wrathful fury or—if I stumbled on the furrows while bringing water to him where he plowed—could shine on me with melting love and manly tenderness.

I see him coming back at evening from the fields with

no sign of tiredness for all his hours of work. Broad, sturdy shoulders taut beneath his shirt robe, his wide white trousers swinging in the straddling gait of the plowman, his thumbs saucily hooked above his thick belt, which sparkles with bright embroidery made by his woman, and around his darkly handsome head his winding turban making a dusty, crooked halo.

His days are spent with the other farmers of Hilwah, exacting from the soil and the seasons, the wheat, the barley, the melons, the cucumbers and corn. But his nights are ours — my mother's and my own — and then, with his feet folded in front of him, he will sit before the fire, his long clay pipe reaching to the floor, and tell the ancient stories and sing the age-old songs.

Often his friends will visit, and then the big sack of sweet-smelling tobacco is laid in the center of their circle so that they may share this aromatic blend which he himself has cut and mixed to his own recipe. Presently someone will notice me standing beside him (though he sits upon the floor, the top of my head is still below his shoulder). "Let Issa try your pipe, Soumay, or he will stay all night sniffing and sniffing." Cocking his head toward mine, he will offer the thin stem to my lips and for the first few times, I will sip on it, reveling in this sudden boon of adulthood until the smoke comes through to fire my mouth and nostrils and sting my tongue with bitterness. I cough and cough. The guests laugh heartily. My father hugs me to his shoulder and suggests that for a while anyway I will have to be content with sniffing, and I agree with him. Completely.

My mother picks me up and brings me to the other room. I look with longing at the large *lehaf* that I had shared with both my parents, but they say I am now big enough for my own bed and for three days my mother has been making it, sifting and sorting the thick wool until a snug, even mattress (*douschack)* has been built between the doubled folds of linen. To that is sewed another, lighter coverlet, and now finished, it is a sheath of downy warmth into which I am slipped. My mother stays awhile to hear my prayers, then

kisses me good-night and returns to her needlework, sitting
on a bright straw mat close to my father's side.

If he has taken down his *oud* (a short-necked gourdlike
lute) that night, then I shall be lullabyed with the melancholy tribal songs of the Kurds as he plucks from it, with a
feather in his fingers, plaintive tales of lost loves found
and heroes fallen.

And I will sleep well, for who knows what adventures
may await me tomorrow? Perhaps my mother will fry the
butter before storing it in the huge jars, and I will watch
the jealous flames licking and snatching the sides of the
skillet. Perhaps she will take some flour to Nisibin to exchange for sugar and dye for her wool, and I will go along
to see the sights and taste the pungency of that exotic, time-
worn city where the palaces of forgotten Aramean-Syrian
kings are crumbled ruins; where Romans, Parthians, and
Persians after them plundered and pillaged and passed into
history. Or perhaps, if it is the proper season, we shall
even go to Basibrina in the mountains, where my mother's
people live, or to Midyat, where my father's people live.
Each harvesting, they share with her the bounty of their
hills, and our donkey returns laden with fat brown grapes
and figs, fruits and nuts. On a journey such as that, we will
see many things: the fields being irrigated as they have
been for centuries with teams of mules driving the water-
wheel that gulps at the edge of the river; white-bearded
men spinning with old-fashioned looms in the open air;
the brilliant raspberry-red robes of the Muslim women en
route to the marketplace. "Women are not as shy as they
once were," so my father says, for they no longer cast their
eyes downward or cover their faces when we pass; instead,
they nod and smile, taking care to balance the wide-
brimmed pastel-tinted pots they carry on their heads. On
the paths outside the towns, they will be barefooted, for
their shoes — a piece of leather and a strap — are tied across
their shoulders until they reach their home or destination.
If we should go, my mother too will carry hers across the
plain in the same fashion; both the life of the desert and

the life of the mountains are teachers par excellence of economy, and our life, our Hilwah, lies between the two.

I plead with her throughout the morning, but this is no day for journeys or a child's meandering adventures. The wheat is piled high on the threshing floors, and the people will want their flour. I will help my mother spread the grain in a great circle. The women will adjust the heavy wooden cylinder and straighten the sharp blades projecting from it. Then the oxen or the donkeys will be hitched and begin their long rotation. Slowly but surely, the straw will separate from the grain, which the woman will sweep up for winnowing; the straw will be sheathed for kindling fuel and livestock fodder during the long, oncoming winter. My duty will be to prod the donkeys onward, for they are rascals and would as soon munch upon the wheat as turn the thresher. They could be muzzled, but that would stain a tradition honored since Biblical times, and a small boy with a long stick can sufficiently serve the purpose.

That evening, I scramble onto my father's back as he sits puffing his pipe near the fire, for I want to boast to him of my work on the threshing floors.

"Bah," he says with gentle mockery. "That is not work, boy. That is why women do it. That is play. Don't worry, soon enough you will work—in the fields with me or by the great waterwheels. These are your years to play, to learn your prayers and how to honor God. When you are old enough and strong enough, then I will tell you, and we shall work together, you and I."

And that was how the cycle of the days and seasons spun around my little home in Hilwah. After nearly rainless summers, when all but the arduously irrigated fields were parched and dry, autumn brought welcome showers, and in November, the Bedouins, longstanding friends and partners in our flocks, encamped briefly about a mile off from the farmlands, and the sheep were entrusted to their care for the winter. Not many days after they had departed for the warmer climates and the scrub grass of the desert's rim, the rains lashed wickedly across the plains and hail-

stones spattered in the empty sheepfold. The nights grew
raw and bitter, though the stormy days were often inter-
spersed with temperate spells of sunshine that sent the
village boys to battle in the cold, dry, radiant snow. Christmas, and my birthday, joyfully came and went; the storms
changed again to showers; verdant patches of grass shot
up along the sun-bleached courtyard wall; the flowers
bloomed.

And then one long-awaited day, a tiny speck upon the
flat horizon to the south is seen to move. Someone working in the moist, plowed earth lets up a shout. And another.
Person after person passes it back to the village. The
woman grasps the child's hand; the farmer halts his plow
midway along the furrow. Dogs yipe excitedly. The aga, or
mayor of the village, is called with hurrying cries. The
Bedouins are returning with the flocks!

Now one can forget the crop assessments levied so
harshly and so soon, forget the frequent hunger of the
winter, and cease to mourn the many who did not survive
it. Today there is only happiness abroad in Hilwah; the
Bedouins are back and there can be no doubt that spring
is here at last. Ironically, on one such splendid day, I was
to hear for the first time the very distant rumblings of war.

Time and brevity of memory steal from my mind his
name, but it is with undimmed affection that I remember
my Bedouin friend.

"But how have you grown so much taller than I in just
one winter?" I ask.

"I am seasons older than you, Issa, and I work hard and
eat as much as a man does."

I grinned to hear my name spoken in Arabic. "And my
father's flock? Did you take good care of it?"

The lanky arm of the young Bedouin circled my shoulder
as he guided me proudly among the noisy sheep and the
fresh, cottony lambs. "After my tribe's share is taken, he
will have twenty-eight more to shear than he had before
the winter came."

I tried to count upon my fingers, but even with both

hands there were not enough to match the figure. "Is that a great many?"

"Not as many as there might have been, but troops of Turkish soldiers demanded tribute so that we might pass. Can you believe that, Issa! The desert has been the home of my people since the moon first rose from the sea, but the insolent Turks say where and when we may cross upon it."

"If I were you," I said haughtily, "I would not have given them any sheep at all."

The Bedouin shook his head in astonishment at the ignorance of the little Syrian fellah. "Then your bones would be bleaching today in the desert." Wide-eyed, I stared up at him. "Issa," he continued, "do you learn anything at all when I am not here? The Turks are at war, boy. At war with many great nations from far away. Why, they will kill anyone who crosses their path."

I caught sight of my father among the farmers dividing the sheep. "Papa," I called, "Papa! There is a war now, and the Turks are killing people."

My father looked from me to the Bedouin youth beside me and sidestepping the oafish sheep, he crossed to us.

"Do not fill a child's head with terrible stories, young Sheikh," he said kindly, and then he addressed me: "Yes, the Turks have been at war all winter long but not with poor farmers or little boys. There is nothing for you to worry about." He wiped his damp forehead with his sleeve and took a miniature braided belt from inside his tunic. "Here. Go join your mother and help her to huddle our flock. Our sheep will each have a collar around its neck marked just as this one is. Now, go along."

I did as I was told but noticed that Soumay stayed behind a moment thoughtfully stroking his moustache — those black, silky wings that curved into his beard — as he listened to the Bedouin, and when I met him again among the sheep, I saw that a troubled preoccupation had settled upon my father's face.

That evening, when the Bedouins had set up camp,

the village feted their nomadic partners. The Sheikh, of
course, dined at the house of the aga, but other tribesmen
sat with Soumay and tasted Khatoun's stew of fresh young
veal while their black-robed women were served *burghul*
in the courtyard. Gaily colored trays of woven straw all
about were piled high with huge walnuts and plump grapes
from Basibrina. Then the men smoked their pipes, the
clays and narghiles (water pipes) too, until the room grew
cloudy and aromatic with sweet herbs, and outside, the
women, in monosyllabic shyness, expressed their approval
of Khatoun's new baby boy who had come like a lamb in the
springtime.

I learned from an Arab guest that my friend had stayed
at camp to herd their goats; I left the smoke- and talk-
filled room, passed among the quieter women, and slipped
through the courtyard gate and out of the village.

The early moon looked like the blade of a silver scimitar
suspended above the distant mountain crags, but even in
the reassuring light it was not without some trepidation
that I approached the ghostly bivouac of the nearly deserted
Bedouin camp.

A semicircle of black tents rose up from the flat land and
a dry, warm breeze slapping at their folds inhabited them
in my mind with a dozen dark assassins. I searched for
my friend with hurried caution. Between the tents, along
the sides pegged to the ground, heaps of melons and sacks
of wheat and barley were discernible. Recognizing the
wide-striped woolen sacks, I knew that these were gifts
or barterings from Hilwah and felt less alien among them.
But then a water-filled goatskin hanging above me moved
in the wind, becoming for an instant a phantom's corpseless
head. This sent me racing through the campsite, scaring
up squawking chickens and raising the dogs to bark.

Outside the encampment, I whirled to find my direction
and nearly sprawled across a low stockade of thornbushes
and sandbags. The sleepy goats therein bleated in alarm.
Then I heard warm laughter flood the night and turned to
find the Bedouin beside me.

"What is it, little farmer?" he asked. "Have you seen Saladin's ghost?"

We pressed each other's open palms by way of greeting and sat down upon the ridge of scrub grass, adjusting our robes and turbans to protect them best from the dusty winds. A loose fold was pulled from the turban—the Bedouin wore the requisite white of the Muslim, I, a darker shade of mottled brown—passed over nose and mouth, and tucked behind a band of woven goat hair. We brought our knees up beneath our chins, and allowed each sleeve to overlap the other. Safely muffled now, we turned to talk.

"The men around my father's fire speak of Turks and war."

"And so they should," the Bedouin said simply. "Is this what you've come so far at night to tell? I shook my covered head. "Then what, little farmer?"

"I was thinking you might stay in Hilwah here with me." The Bedouin leaned back and laughed softly at the moon. "But what if you should meet more Turks?" I insisted. "More sinful Turks who—who said—you crossed their path?"

A dusky hand eased from the sleeve of the Bedouin's robe and comforted my shoulder. "They woo my people, Issa," he told me. "They seek our knowledge of the desert in their war. They threaten, even raise their swords in anger, but they will not harm those whom they need to serve them."

"But—*you*—will not serve them, will you?"

The Bedouin clicked his tongue. "That will depend on what they offer in return. The saying is, 'Whose bread I eat, his songs alone I sing.'"

I hoped he was joking but could not be certain, for the cross cloth cut off all except the Bedouin's dark eyes.

But after a moment, the Bedouin laughed again. "No, Issa, I will not serve them. Nor will my people. They would order us perhaps to murder Christians, and the Bedouin is friend to the Christian; we journey in the same direction, though we travel by different trails."

My forehead puckered in confused thoughts. "But the Turks," I said. "Are they not Muslim with the Bedouins?"

The youth nodded his head. "But they have departed from the precepts of the Book." In a flash, he whipped a short curved dagger from his waistband and sent it whizzing toward a nearby shrub of furze. It found its mark and deftly pinned a scorpion and stayed poised in the branch, its ram's horn handle ticking like an exhortatory finger. "Departed from the precepts of the Book," he said again, going to reclaim his knife. "And they will feel the wrath of Allah soon."

Later, when others returned to the camp, the Bedouin lifted me into his arm and carried me back to the village.

The "wrath of Allah" had subtly been moving against the Turkish despots for many years. The once fantastically expanded Ottoman Empire had begun declining as far back as the Russo-Turkish Wars a century before. The north and northeastern coasts of the Black Sea were lost then along with the long-subjected nations of Greece and Egypt. That century, too, saw Bosnia and Serbia, Romania and Montenegro, Bulgaria and the Isle of Crete, escape from the Turk's cruel grip. Revolts, corruption, and staggering public debts corroded the remaining empire from within, and when Enver Pasha, the satanically handsome leader of the Young Turks, acquired dictatorial powers in 1909–1910, though he promised peace, prosperity, and equal rights to all his subjects, neither his own citizens nor the representatives of foreign governments shared these illusions for a moment. In Khíos, in 1822, nearly the entire Greek population fell under Turkish swords; in 1876, thousands of Bulgarians were slaughtered on the suspicion of an intended uprising; in 1895, more than a hundred thousand Armenian Christians were martyred by Abdul-Hamid rather than abjure their ancient faith. True, Pasha and his Young Turks had deposed Hamid and presented themselves to the world as benevolent apostles of freedom, but the taste for blood and violence is an intoxicating inheritance not easily denied, especially if this addiction finds firm support from a stalwart companion, and imperial Germany provided such a friend.

Germany hoped for colonies in Asia Minor. By an awesome exercise of her national imagination, she envisioned restoring Mesopotamia to its richness of ages past, but under her codes and people. She hoped to accomplish this by a land highway and railroad which would finally connect directly Hamburg, Constantinople, Baghdad, and the Persian Gulf, and thus diminish the strategic and economic importance of Russia's railways and the English sea-lanes through the Suez Canal. Furthermore, such a tremendous line of supply and communication would have German power flanking Persia, dominating Arabia, and pointing like an arrow at the very vitals of India.

Britain was quick to sense her vast Eastern interests endangered here. Russia likewise saw a threat to the richest portion of her empire at its most vulnerable part, and the Dardanelles Strait was Russia's only shipping egress not rendered icebound by her treacherous winters. For years, these combustibles had been bouncing around in the halls of diplomacy. Now, with the rest of the world exploding, they were ignited, at last set ablaze. And Mesopotamia was circled by their fires.

I stirred as my mother kissed me and tucked the coverlet of my *lehaf* under my chin. The accent of tobaccos still haunted the rooms sweetly, and my father stood in the doorway humming a slow, soft song.

And my dreams that night were vivid with anticipations. I could foresee already my *own* green plot of land, my own little house and fireside in Hilwah. I could imagine the mutual, expansive pride of walking down the early morning byways with my father as he had done with *his* father, and he with his father before him.

But neither the schemes of history nor the designs of God's often inscrutable will reckon with the flights and fancies of a boy's ambition. And God, working through

history, is the one who is the final architect of all our
houses.

They were far off—a thin, dark graph inching across the
shimmering white horizon. They had come down from the
hill country, so they were not Bedouins. Nor could one
distinguish any camels in the caravan. Larger images, men
on horses probably, moved at the sides and the rear of the
gatherings. Who they were, where they were going, moving so slowly into the desert, we did not know, but often I
and my playmates in the field surrounding Hilwah would
look up from our games and wonder.

As the heat of the summer blistered such ground as was
not watered and the sky turned copper around a bloody
sun, these ominous processions appeared more frequently
and we learned that they were Armenians. Colonists, we
were told, who were en route to newly established settle-
ments along the Tigris somewhere between Mosul and
the fabled Baghdad.

They were not willing colonists. Sometimes at night, in
the still, stunned darkness of the desert, their cries would
thread the dry winds with dirgelike music. And the day
finally came when one such tribe passed right near us.

In command were a few Turks, baleful giants of men
astride gaunt, sweating horses. When they rode into the
village demanding "donations" of supplies from every
household, the coils of whip hanging from their saddle
horns were caked with dried blood.

The people of Hilwah protested. If their brethren the
Armenians needed food, they would share what little they
had; however, they wished to take it directly to the caravan.
But the Turks insisted that they were soldiers—though
they wore no military uniforms—with full authority from
the Mustafsherif to collect such "donations" by force if
necessary. "If your village does not comfort them," they
added, "they will surely starve to death in the desert. Do
you wish their fate on your strange Christian consciences?"

The villagers had no choice. Perhaps the Armenians

would get *some* of it. One by one they returned to their
homes and brought forth from their own stores and supplies—already meager through heavy taxations—sacks of
flour, lumps of sugar, and clusters of thin, dried figs. A
farmer's cart was confiscated as a transport and the Turks
returned to their "colonists."

From the edge of the fields we watched them pass.
There were perhaps a hundred people, old people mostly,
and only a few were men. They hardly looked at us. When
they did, no sign of recognition lighted their dark, vacant
eyes. Only one child, a blond child, a girl younger than
myself, smiled in lunatic delight at everything around her.
The other faces were clouded in hopelessness and the
solemnity of death.

We had heard rumors, and more rumors, and much
propaganda as counterbalance. But now we had *seen*.

That evening, after silent, unrelished suppers, as if by
intuition the villagers assembled together in the church to
pray—for the poor creatures who had passed that afternoon,
for our continued safety, and for a world gone insane
with war. As we neared the end of the service the road
through Hilwah rattled with galloping horsehoofs and the
raucous cries of drunken riders. A crash of splintering
wood startled the congregation, and men went outside to
find the confiscated cart, empty now and shattered against
the side of the building. And the calm of the night was
rent with the wild shrieks and blasphemies of northbound
Turks.

In the morning, the farmers found one survivor who had
somehow straggled back to the town to tell of an orgy of
slaughter on the desert's sand.

He was a cripple with a shriveled arm and leg that had
exempted him from military service, and he was not quite
as old as the others in his convoy, which had given him
the strength to crawl away in the darkness.

"You were right," he told the elders after he had been
bathed and fed. "Your supplies were for themselves alone.
It was never intended that we should reach colonies near

Baghdad or even Mosul. Nor were they soldiers. They do not waste Young Turks on old Armenians. These men and all the others like them are criminals released from jail expressly to escort us to the desert—to our death."

For a moment, the men squatted around him in incredulous silence. "But there have been caravans such as this by the hundreds since the spring. And there must have been thousands of people. Surely some reached the colonies safely."

A haggard smile creased the cripple's face. He shook his head. "There are no colonies. There never were. In Trezibond when they started, no one saw anyone killed, but a few days after the Armenians left the city, their bodies came floating down the river. The deserts serve better the plans of the Turks. What is done there leaves only a rumor over the shifting sand . . . ." He sipped from a bowl of water, relished it in his mouth like some rare wine. "The Turks seek an Armenia without Armenians," he said quietly. "And they will have it."

Then word by grisly word there proceeded from his bitter memory a litany of horror such as had not been heard since the savagery of Genghis Khan was loosed upon the world a thousand years before.

He told of the slaughter of fifty-five thousand Armenians in the area of Lake Van; how conquering Russians had to forbid the eating of all fish caught in that vast body of water because of the multitude of corpses that floated therein. He told of Armenians forced to stand close together so that a single bullet might be made to do the work of four; of mothers throwing infants into the Euphrates in despair and young girls raped before the eyes of helpless brothers or mutilated husbands.

The people were mesmerized with shock. Though the Syrians themselves had had lengthy experience with oppression, torture, and barbaric persecution at the hands of many enemies, and though the once rich fields of Mesopotamia had been with discouraging frequency the scene of many a bloody page in history, they were not quite prepared to believe that such things could occur in the presumably civilized world of 1915. But they did. The people listened and learned and wept with the cripple for his ill-fated nation, that most ancient of Christian states, and when he died a few days later in diseased agony, they attended his body and buried him in holy ground. As it turned out, news was not the only thing that this poor man had brought to Hilwah; cholera had also journeyed with him.

Before the summer's white-hot sands had drifted to the cooler dunes of autumn, the town was ravaged by an epidemic. Corpses turned carrion in the fields before there was time or manpower to bury them. Death registered a threatening guest in every house. It was as though Nature, infuriated at the carnage of the war was determined to prove that she still could be deadlier than humanity.

My father could not believe it. Not a week ago, he had worked his fields, a strong and healthy husband and father in the prime of his life. Now he lay stricken, weakened by a stomach that refused even the thin broth which Khatoun prayerfully spooned past his lips, and at the same time rendered helplessly humiliated by the scourge of uncontrollable excretion. The hand he raised to my shoulder trembled like a reed in the khamsin.

"If God should take me, Yeshue," he said, "you must listen to your mother always. Help her to raise your brother as I had hoped to raise you. If . . ."

But the tears brimming in my eyes above him were contagious. With a mighty exertion, he raised himself up and clasped me to his breast. "Oh, my Yeshue, I will never see you grown tall and strong. Never . . ." His thickened tongue could say no more. His hand fell lifelessly upon the *lehaf*. He turned his face to hide his tears.

He heard Khatoun comforting me, felt cool threads stitching his fevered face, tasted damp saltness through his sanded lips and thought of the green mountains of Midyat and the silken winds of the desert's dawn.

His grave was not a lonely one. Many of his friends and fellow townsmen shared it. In that hill of consecrated ground they await together with joy and patience their promised resurrection.

Later, an elder of the village who had promised my father to look after us came to the house. From his girdle, I saw him take a small brass bottle of ink and a few reed pens. He sharpened the pens and began to make a list of our possessions: the number of our sheep, the quantities of wheat and barley in our bins. I took my little brother outside to the courtyard so as to permit the man to work in peace, and playing with the baby by the *tannour*, I took a stick in hand and scratched upon the earth. What a marvelous accomplishment, I thought, to put a pen to paper and give scratches meaning! For a moment, the very wonder of it encompassed my grief.

In the autumn the Bedouins came for the flocks. Winter followed with long and melancholy nights in which my father's voice no longer cheered the fireside. The oud hung silent upon the wall, unless my mother touched it with a dustcloth, which raised a few sad notes that split our hearts.

Conflicting rumors reached us through the winter. Russia, it was said, held the vast territory between Erzurum in Turkey and Kermanshah in the Persian mountains. The British were reportedly in control of Baghdad, and the Turks would be vanquished before spring. It seemed something to hope for, but in a land that had served as the battleground of empires, in a country successively dominated by Assyrians, Babylonians, Persians, Greeks, Romans, and Arabs, and for the last three centuries by the Turks, the people of Mesopotamian villages such as Hilwah were slow in expressing premature hopes. Their atavistic reluctance was not unfounded.

The returning Bedouins in the spring brought thinned, unhealthy flocks—they had found many of the winter grazing areas proscribed to them. The news they brought was equally distressing. The British had *never* reached Baghdad. Instead, they had been halted in Kut-El-Amara, a hundred miles south of that objective. There they had

spent the winter besieged and had at last surrendered such
starving, wounded soldiers as survived. The Young Turks,
under the guidance of, and reinforced by, German troops,
had also been victorious at Gallipoli and held the vital
strait at Dardanelles. The war was a long way from being
over.

Harvest, 1916, was a spiritless undertaking. A government decree had raised taxes to enormous proportions,
and there was little joy in gathering a field in which an
ominous poster declared it to be the property of "Non-
Turks." And every passing stranger, every mercantile convoy, brought more bitter news of the wanton, wide-scale
slaughter of Armenians; tales of starving half-crazed exiles
eating grass until the fierce, arid days of the Mesopotamian
summer took even that from them and forced the more
desperate to cannibalism or carrion. They told of sick
people throwing themselves into graves and parents killing their children rather than see them delivered up to
the atrocities of the Turks.

The world, too, heard of these things, and the phrase
"the starving Armenians" became a byword in the tongues
of many languages. But those who heard it thought of
people going without a meal or two, or hungry for a fort-
night. They did not envision eyebrows plucked out, breasts
and genitals torn off amidst scornful laughter, nails ripped
from the fingers or spikes driven into men's feet as might
be done with horses. If, for example, the world outside
heard of the massacre in Tel-Armen near Mardin, no doubt
they thought of five thousand soldiers falling in battle;
they could not conceive of five thousand civilians of both
sexes, all ages, being thrown into fires or tossed alive into
wells.

The elders of Hilwah conferred over many a pipe-
clouded hour and though it is doubtful that they knew
such a modern term, they decided evacuation was the only
hopeful solution. One day's steady journey and we would
reach the mountains. Numerous friends and relatives were
there and being more remote, more inaccessible, it was

safer from the war's impending terrors. For many, including my mother, it would mean leaving the aggregates of a
lifetime behind them, but there seemed no sensible alternative. It was agreed we would go from Hilwah.

One autumn evening, the sad caravan made ready.

"As soon as the threshing is finished," Khatoun promised, "I will follow with the other women." And she held
me close to her for just a moment, fearing that too long, too
affectionate an embrace would dissolve us both in weeping.

"But, Mama, why can't you go now? Tonight? There
are others who can do the work."

She held my shoulders firmly as if to pass to me some
measure of her own courage and resolution. "The more
there are to do the work," she explained, "the sooner it
will be finished. It would be foolish to burden ourselves
with both straw *and* grain, Yeshue, when a few days threshing will give us only the flour to carry."

"Then why can't I wait until it's finished? I can work
the donkeys. You know I can do that."

"Because your uncle Joseph needs your help with the
flocks."

I looked up to the tall, thin man beside me. He smiled
in agreement. (His smile was much like Soumay's, for this
was Soumay's brother.) After a moment, I felt resigned.

"But will you come soon, Mama?"

"As soon as possible, my child. A week. Perhaps ten
days. You will not be far. We have gone to the mountains
before, haven't we?"

I nodded. My mother stopped and placed the strap of
my *jirab* around my shoulder. I had never worn one before,
and if I had wanted to cry, it was too late now, for a boy
old enough to have his own goatskin shepherd's bag, plump
with bread and olives and lumps of sugar, could not whimper like a baby, could not squall out his feelings the way
my little brother Malky—peeking from behind his mother's
skirt—was doing now. No, a real shepherd with a real
jirab could not do that—even if he wanted to with all his
heart.

Sheep joggled along beside me, muttering their sleepy discontent. My uncle Joseph had lifted me onto a slowly swaying donkey. Some miles out, we inclined toward a gentle valley, and I turned back to see the town once more. It seemed tranquil and tiny, with small clusters of doll-like homes, white pillboxes with low, domed roofs in moonlit iridescence beneath a black-velvet heaven struck with stars — like a sleeping Bethlehem painted for Christmas cards.

My uncle read my worried thoughts. He patted my knee good-naturedly. "We will be back as soon as the war is over, Yeshue," he said, "and we will once more know happiness and peace in Hilwah."

I smiled, but despite my warm woolen wrappings, a flickering chill ran through me. Could I have somehow guessed that I would never see that town, that home, that fireside again?

Dawn found our wearied caravan ascending the mountain road. It was damp here and quite cool, but the morning sun soon splashed fire through the surrounding oak forests and the young found ripe, meaty walnuts to collect from the roadside.

By midmorning, we had left the forest behind us and were hedged in by the inhospitable crags and cliffs of the higher mountains. Far below, deep slicing valleys — in springtime cloudy with the pinks and purples of abundant blossoming fruit trees — were lifeless canyons starkly awaiting winter. Even the village of Khirbet-Eli, which we had just passed, seemed ominously deserted with its little houses of sunbaked earth and thatched roofs lying silent in the sun. No *tannour* smoked, though one could see beside them the carefully stored piles of dried dung, fuel that would become more precious as the winter months progressed, and no women dallied near the well to gossip as they filled their water jars.

The members of our caravan observed the scene with sullen curiosity. No one ventured an opinion, but the contagious thought settled upon us like an invisible disquieting fog: Surely the war and its terrors had not reached this far into the mountains!

The first shot hit a sheep, sent it rolling, reeling, bleating down the steepness of the valley.

My uncle and the other men shouted everyone back against the mountainside. The shot had come from above us and the overhanging crags were our only shields. Women and girls were made to stay flat against the wall of the mountain while the boys herded the flocks and pack animals as close to them as possible.

Another shot and another shredded the morning's calmness, pocking the roads and the rocks around us. The men dug into packs and saddlebags and produced a number of weapons, but they were old and rusty and only a few proved usable. In the excitement, one of my younger lambs dodged from the flock and out into the unshadowed road. I started after it, but my uncle caught my shoulder and held me back.

"Stay under, Yeshue," he ordered. "They will not purposely kill a lamb but they might think a boy worth a bullet."

"Is it Turks? Have the Turks followed us?" I asked.
He shook his head. "I do not think so."

"Then who? Who else would shoot at us?"

He glanced toward the protecting cliffs. "Kurds," he said quietly. "Kurds."

"But why, Uncle?"

Men toward the front of the dissembled caravan were calling Uncle Joseph to join them.

"They may be attacking us because we are Christians," he told me quickly. "Or to steal our few small possessions."

The others called him again. He signaled that he was coming. There was no time for lessons in history. A few steps away, though, he turned and smiled broadly; it was the same forebearing grin my father had displayed in the face of trouble. "Perhaps," he called, "they just had nothing else to do this morning."

A nomadic mountain people, as I would later learn, the

Kurds were unevenly dispersed throughout vast regions stretching from Russian Transcaucasia far south into Russia and Iraq. As ancient Aryans, they had descended from the steppes east of the Caspian Sea about 1500 B.C., a fierce race of frequently red-headed or blond and blue-eyed people in a world of more darkly tinted Semites. Once the privileged guardians of Zoroastrian temples, they are for the most part now devout Muslims of the Sunnite sect, for whom the murder or robbery of an "infidel Christian" was, in the days of which I write, of no greater consequence than the crushing of a flea caught in the folds of a turban.

During the heat of noon, the hitherto sporadic shooting ceased altogether. Our caravan huddled closely, and the elders led us in prayer. If we did not get past them or defeat them by nightfall, there was little hope we could survive the hours of darkness in these unfamiliar and forboding mountains.

One young man who had volunteered to reconnoiter returned with encouraging news. He had not been able to determine how many there were opposing us or where they were at the moment, but within a half hour's walk there was an ancient monastery, and surrounding its courts and vineyards were the walls of a veritable fortress. It was well situated and probably inhabited, though he had not been close enough to be certain of the latter. But if the Kurds did take up their assault during the afternoon, they would probably leave off again at sundown for prayers and the evening meal, and we might then, with the help of Almighty God, be able to reach the monastery.

God was with us. That evening, unobserved in the descending darkness, we attained the Monastery of St. Malky.

"We should like to stay the night, good brother," an elder entreated. The grizzled old monk who had cautiously unbarred the huge wooden gate did not reply. "There are a dozen or more Kurds who have kept us all day under assault."

The monk nodded wearily and strained to pull back the heavy oaken door. "Not a *dozen*," he grumbled. "A hundred dozen. Perhaps a thousand dozen. And they have given us no peace in as many days."

We entered to find the great courtyard of the monastery a panorama of disorder: dirty-faced children ran unrestricted amid muddled flocks of sheep and goats; dour women cooked in groups over small begrudging fires; men slept against the wall or stretched out straight upon the ground, some still grasping rifles tightly in their muscled hands. Our leaders paused, stunned at the sight before them.

"Get in. Get in," the old monk grunted. "We may as well all die tomorrow as tonight. Let me seal the door."

A few other monks joined him, nodding weary welcomes. But we knew from their faces that each new guest, each additional lamb or pack animal, incensed even more the cupidity of the Kurds. The monks fulfilled their Christian duty by granting us sanctuary, but their human natures could not entirely disregard the fact that our presence could only serve to increase the wrath of the enemy.

"Your people may have this portion of the courtyard," a young monk told us. He roused up a number of sheep. "It is not clean, but there is little space left. If they continue through the winter, we will make room inside for you, though the sick and wounded already crowd the halls."

Too tired to worry about the future, we settled down as best we could and slept.

And this was only the first of many, many nights through which we would sleep fitfully on the stones of St. Malky's, unwilling combatants in yet another war—one which history would probably not warrant worth recording. But from common suffering came mutual consideration, and as winter drew on, despite want and privation, a noble sense of fellowship manifested itself. Our sheep, along with the others, for example, were herded into common flocks and those which did not die were slaughtered as needed for food. Man and monk, merchant and farmer, mountaineer and plainsmen, all become brothers relying on God and each other to see them through.

During the days, the women and children huddled tensely inside the monastery itself, listening to the whining bullets that assailed the courtyard. At night, the monks led us in prayer while some slipped off to bury our dead covertly in the darkness. Malnutrition underwrote death's invitation while diarrhea, pneumonia, and infections passed from sheep to men, and untreatable battle wounds supplied the final requirements. The ditches were more quickly filled with the victims of disease than with the victims of this senseless, isolated mountain war.

Christmas came and went, unmarked by happiness. The fierce winter of these high altitudes discouraged many of the Kurdish warriors, but some persisted in hope of inevitable victory.

Men from our feeble company went out each day on guerrilla raids, but their ammunition, mostly bullets made of brass dishes and spoons that the monks had melted down, was ineffective, their successes few and costly. Never as many returned as had gone out.

My bloated face a vivid yellow, I sat staring into the darkness. The monks were kind, one in particular shared his own ration with me every day, but there was no Ossyo here and the nearest real doctor, so they said, was far off at the American Hospital in distant Mardin. Fear, as much as jaundice, gnawed at my vitals. Grim rumors fed my fevered mind: many Syrians of the Tour-Abdeen district had been killed. The towns of Midyat and Ain-Ward had resisted, and the entire population, including their bishops, priests, and monks, had been massacred. No news came that was cheering, and communication with my mother was impossible. There was only one smattering of joy in all my life—that moment after nightfall when my uncle returned from battle to hold me for a moment, stroking my hot brow with rough but soothing fingers, whispering

words of consolation and of hope, provoking the only smile
of the day.

A wind had risen sharply. The old monk at the gate bade
me to join the others who had gone within. I declined,
explaining that I always waited for the men to return, and
added an assurance that I was not really cold.

At last, after what seemed a very long cold time, despite
the whistle of the wind and the woolen scarf tight about
my ears, I heard the coded knock. Twice. Twice again.
Three times.

The old monk, wheezing, shuffled to the gate and raised
the bar. The men entered. One. Two. Three. Disheartened.
Hungry. Cold. Their eyes cast down, they did not regard
me. Four. Five. *He* was patient, Uncle Joseph; he would
be the last. Six. Six . . . six.

The monk peered out, grimacing at the night. Then
wordlessly he pulled the great door to and lowered the
oaken bar. I ran to him. "Only six, monk! Only six came
back! Nine, or ten perhaps, went out this morning!"

"Then that is all there is," the monk said simply.

"But my uncle—he wasn't among them, was he? My
uncle Joseph—did he come back?"

"I do not ask their names," the old monk muttered. "Go
within and see yourself who's there and who is not."

And I turned and ran toward the men entering the dark
monastery but even as I neared them, I knew the answer.
My eyes, jaundiced as they were, did not deceive me. My
uncle would not be "within." Only the somber mountains
knew where he lay among their snow-stacked crags. And
the mountains would not speak.

The people from Hilwah commiserated with me, but
there was little else they could do. My infirmity added to
the burden of supplying my food, and the laws of survival
were becoming more and more pronounced, sowing selfish-
ness in the kindest of hearts and self-interest in the most
altruistic. Food rations had to be guarded constantly.
Hunger stretched all ethical considerations to the limit.

Only the monks, sickly themselves and further depleted in stores by the impossibility of collecting their traditional donations of bread from neighboring households, only they maintained any genuinely Christian standards.

One monk took me beneath his wing. In our early days he had been a rounded jolly fellow, but now the unfed flesh sagging from his jowls and cheekbones gave him the features of a weary Saint Bernard dog.

Each day he made certain that I had food and water. Frequently, I think, it was his own. And as much from his infectious goodness as from the nutrients he made available, I began to feel my health returning.

"Now, Yeshue, you seem well enough this morning to do some work."

"Do, I, Brother?"

"You do, indeed. And there is much to be done. A new monk arrived yesterday with fearful news. Only God's protection carried him this far safely."

"What news?"

"The Monasteries of St. Gabriel and St. Augain have been sacked and robbed. The tombs of the saints are desecrated, and most of the monks have been murdered."

"But what can *we* do, Brother?"

"We can pray and have faith in the mercy of Our Lord. And we can also bury our books. Come on, now. Rise up. Good boy. It is time that you tasted adventure."

We were not outside the monastery three minutes when an alert but invisible Kurd noted our movements. Bullets spattered the ancient stone wall behind us, and as a body, two monks, three other boys, and myself, vaulted into a nearby gully. On hands and knees we made our way swiftly out of his range.

About a half mile from the gateway, we came upon a flattened hillside slope, more earthen than rock. The monk in front paused. "Here," he said. "This is the place."

From inside his jubbah he produced a well-worn manuscript, the many colors of its elaborate lettering faded like old pressed flowers. Then another, and another, until a considerable bundle lay before us on the ground.

Meanwhile, the other monk had scraped a circle into the winter-hardened earth and gestured to us to take stone and stick and help him hollow it. My strength was feebly matched with the work of digging, but the excitement served as stimulant. Occasional rifle shot whizzed overhead, sending us to our knees to take cover and to pray.

"Should we take time to pray, Brothers?" one of the older boys asked. "Kneeling down and in one spot, we are excellent targets here."

The monks considered this for a moment. Then the once jolly one replied, "If I am going to be shot, young fellah, I should prefer to be at my prayers when it is done." Then he had us ask the blessed saints to intervene on our behalf and even to shorten, if God willed, these days of terror. Fearful the saints might act upon this last suggestion, we commenced digging with revitalized enthusiasm and in no time at all the hole was wide and deep enough.

Carefully, the manuscripts were placed therein and the aperture sealed with pitch. Then rocks and stones and earth were blended over it to perfectly conceal it. "There," said the monk. "Now *let* them raze the monastery. Those who follow after us will have our records and our books of liturgy to guide them. The work of God will prevail."

"As always," the jolly monk added.

"Amen," the other said curtly.

Later, comparatively safe in the courtyard, I looked up at this friendly monk in awe. "But today, Brother, when the shooting seemed so close to us, were you never once afraid?"

"I relied on the mercy and grace of God, Yeshue. He was the source of my courage." He cupped his hand under my chin. "The mortal man in me, though, was as frightened as a rabbit, and starving to death, by the way."

He walked off among the sick and widowed, dispensing water and kind words. He was that combination of simplicity and greatness, of sublimity and human frailty, from which heroes are made. And saints.

As spring approached, the Kurds apparently found other distractions, for their raids diminished considerably. But jaundice and influenza did not abandon *their* assaults. Stricken again with the yellow sickness, I was taken very low and realized a few days after this renewed attack that I had somehow also lost the use of my legs.

"But we cannot wait for his recovery, Brother," one of the Hilwah elders told the monk. "Each day means life to us. We must take advantage of this lull in battle and seek out our own again. Who knows but that the Kurds will return tomorrow in force? Perhaps, finding us gone, they will leave your vineyards and your monastery in peace."

The monks conferred with one another. What the elder had spoken was true. Still, I had arrived with them and they were my only link with my own kinfolk and my home. If they could not wait until I could walk by myself again, they would have to bear me with them on a litter. This agreed upon, a blanket and poles were fetched to fashion a crude stretcher.

I forced my eyes to stay closed. Bitterly self-conscious of the burden I had become, I could not bear to look at the men who carted me so clumsily along the mountain road. At a cattle well on the outskirts of Khirbet-Eli, the company stopped for water. I was thirsty too, but ashamed to ask for yet another favor.

"Is he asleep?" I heard a gruff voice ask.

"Not a sign from him since we left the monks," another replied. And still another said: "He is dead — or dying, anyway."

The gruff voice was lowered, speaking confidentially to those beside him: "Perhaps we should leave him here."

"Yes," whispered another. "He will only slow us down."

"And surely die before we reach Basibrina."

I was freezing, and did not dare to breathe. My mouth was suddenly as dry and coarse as the wool wrapped around me.

"He will be better here. They may have pity on him."

"Believe me, he will not live the day in any case."

Ah, now, a woman's voice protested: "How will you face Khatoun?"

And silence answered until the gruff voice spoke again: "He may be joining her. Who knows what horrors have befallen Hilwah?"

It was decided. In my panic and my pride, I did not open my eyes until the last departing footfall echoed far down the mountain road.

Above me the sun, a flaming rose, spun blindingly. About a hundred feet away the village pool, a low stone well intended for livestock use, bubbled innocently in the warm springlike morning. If I could only drink, I thought, I would feel better. But hunger and the debility of jaundice and influenza had depleted me. I tried to crawl, but my arms would not support my weight. I fell back upon the stretcher without strength enough to weep. Then, mercifully, I slept.

The shooting woke me. The sun was out of sight now and the area seemed to be under a continuous rain of rifle fire. Who or why it was I did not know, but night became a time of terror as I watched the weird reflections of bursting shells in the undulating waters of the pool. Wild jackals returned my most quiet whimper in a hideously distorted echo; what angels kept them from making a meal of me I may never know.

The hours crept by. The darkness and the chill of night acted as a brief restorative, and during a cessation of firing, I dragged myself to the poolside and brought those welcome waters to my cracked, parched lips. Then I crawled back and pulled the blanket from the stretcher into a cramping shelter of roadside rocks.

The jackals mocked me from the surrounding hills. If I had my sling, I thought, I would show them. They would not be so arrogant if I had my sling. . . . I had used it once to shoot at birds in the fields of Hilwah—small birds that meant no harm. Perhaps this was a punishment . . . perhaps that was why I did not have it now.

I thought of the sheep I was so fond of pasturing, of childhood companions playing in the sun. And of my mother. Mother—when she was through at the threshing floors, would she still seek me . . . and in vain? Hunger—and recurring chills and fever. A leaden dawn began to usurp the heavens.

The heavens . . . God had made them just as he had made me. Was he finished with me already? *I relied on the mercy and grace of God,* the monk had said happily. Was there mercy in this lingering death? I tried to pray but could not organize my thoughts sufficiently.

The sun was high again and hot. I searched my memory and tried to find some source of strength and sustenance, and at last recalled a question and an answer from my catechism class in the little church in Hilwah. Adam had just been expelled from Paradise.

Did God abandon man?

No. He showed mercy on him and promised him a Savior that would come.

I repeated the answer again and again until the words became gibberish. Then I slept feverishly and Kronos devoured the children of this second day.

That night I drank again at the pool. The shooting was distant now, and the hope that I might even fall into Kurdish hands had vanished. A scrawny dog approached, barked, and sniffed at me. Then, as indifferently as the wind, he ambled off and I was alone again.

On the morning of the third day I was so weak I could not raise myself to crawl. Thick mucous coated my mouth and throat, and I had not power enough to salivate or swallow. Fever and starvation pushed me close to the rim of madness.

Did God abandon man? No. He showed mercy on him and promised him a Savior that would come.

Hazily, I could see a face. A beard on it. And blackness all around. Blackness—though beyond, the afternoon sun was bright. The beard moved. Lips above it. Words inched through the buzz of pain.

"Child . . ." the words said, "poor, poor child. . . . I thought . . . a little animal . . . hunched up . . . What . . . ? How did . . .?" And I felt strong, warm hands sliding under my back, felt myself lifted higher, higher, become an airy thing, as though all matter fell away as I was lifted. The blackness vanished, the sun all bright again. *Did God abandon man? No. He showed mercy . . .*

As he carried me along my senses returned. He was a priest, and the blackness had been his robe. He took me to his home, and after his wife had given me fresh milk and butter, they listened to my story and wept with me unashamedly.

"Mary," he told his wife, "we have long prayed for a child. Perhaps, for a while at least, God has answered our prayer."

In the warmth of a newly made *lehaf,* with milk and fruit and hot bread in abundance, I seemed to have found the paradise my Bedouin friends dreamed of. Slowly, life seeped back into my frail body, and my arms and legs gradually fleshed out, but it was as an infant, stumbling, that I learned again how to walk.

Father Demetrius owned a vineyard in addition to a goodly number of goats and a healthy flock of sheep. After I was fully recovered, I would often go with him to the vineyard to guard it from the poaching fox and jackal.

There was a solid dry wall around it and at its center a squat stone tower with stairs leading to the top. The entry could be blocked from the inside, and once he reached the crenellated circle of its turret, a boy felt that he could hold the world at bay.

Through the long nights we would take separate watches, though I often ended mine asleep at the foot of the patient priest, who would carry me back to my morning bed without even waking me up. They were gracious nights, dark and deep, and each one warmer than the last. The stars came to look upon us as old friends, and the verdant earth softly breathed forth her sweetness to sting our nostrils and lightly wound our hearts with the wonder of April and living things.

He continued me in my catechism. "Question: When did Christ begin his public life?"

"Christ began his public life at the age of—"

"Of thirty years."

"Of thirty years, when he was baptized by Saint John in the river—ah—"

"What river?"

"Euphrates?"

"Yeshue, the Euphrates isn't the only river in the world, you know."

"No, Father."

"Now, what river?"

"The—ah—ah—Tigris!"

"No. No. No. The Jordan. The Jordan. Can you never remember that?"

"The Jordan."

"Yes." And he would chuckle and tousle my hair. "Ah, Yeshue, shall we ever make a proper Christian of you, son?"

Nightly, we would pray for my father's soul and my mother's safekeeping. We heard nothing of Hilwah. Only the most urgent news of the great War managed to reach us.

"A General Maude," the priest announced one night in the tower, "an English gentleman, has taken Baghdad. That is an important success, Yeshue. And they say the Anglo-Indian forces are this side of the Sinai Desert. Soon they will cut the Ottoman Empire right down the center and the Turks will be defeated."

I stretched lazily, reaching for the stars. I was still appallingly thin, but my frame had added cubits since the vanished winter. "I hope so, Father," I said. "I hope they cut the empire into a *thousand* pieces."

For a moment only, the night sounds ticked between us. Then I heard the priest speak in a low, uncommonly serious tone. "You must never hate, Yeshue. Never. Indeed, you *cannot* hate and call yourself a Christian."

I turned. The war's sufferings and indignities, my own and those of others, give my convictions pertinence. "But the Young Turks, the soldiers at least, surely we must hate them."

Slowly, the priest moved his head from side to side.

"Have you ever *thought* about the Young Turks, Yeshue? I mean as human beings, not as enemies? Think of them, boy. Look out there over the dark vineyards and think of them. They have parents from whom they are separated, just as you are. They have hopes and dreams and fevers and fleas like every one of us. An empire goes to war and the Young Turk has no course but to follow. He knows no alternative, and to flee from it would be cowardice and treason. And so he goes to war for his rulers.

"The distances in the desert are enormous, his means of transportation very poor. He subsists and marches obediently and fights with all his might on next to nothing. He has no provision train, no commissary as his rival soldiers have. A cup of coffee, a handful of barley or corn, sometimes only a drop of water and a few dates, must last him for days at a time. His weapons are old. Often his leaders are stupid and untrained. Yet he tries to do what he has been commanded, whether the khamsin blows or the rain pours down in torrents when his tent is patched and ragged —if indeed, he is so fortunate as to have a tent.

"No, Yeshue, he is to be pitied perhaps, but not without a drop of sympathy and even admiration. Hate the war, yes, and the savagery in which it permits man to indulge, but look for reasons to love the man himself. For God has made him your brother, and Christ has died to save you both. Look for reasons to love, Yeshue, and you'll always find them."

I did not reply. I stared up at the incomprehensible heavens, stricken with awe at such a loving God who would offer his only Son—and even for the Turks.

In the mornings we would walk back hand in hand from the vineyard. Father Demetrius never tired of finding in a sunrise or a cloud shape or a flock of pasture-bound sheep some aspect of the beauty with which God filled the world for those who took time to see it. As we neared the house the sharp mountain air carried the heady scent of baking bread. Mary would be smiling by the *tannour,* deftly peeling the smoking, pancake-shaped loaves from its interior.

"The vinters are home," the young priest would call to her. "They are home and they are hungry." And as though she had a genie, within minutes she would put before us cool milk and soft warm bread, cheeses and fresh fruit.

Mary and Father Demetrius overwhelmed me with affection and provided me for the first time in many months with "a fullness of bread and prosperous ease." But my proper home, of course, was with my mother and my brother, and the good priest constantly asked in the little hamlets of his mountain parish after any news that would allay my concern over their fate. "One day, Yeshue," he would say cheerfully, "one day soon, God willing, we shall hear something." And one day, we did.

There could be no doubt—it was spring. Every whisper of the breeze shook from the blossoming olive trees a flurry of snowy flowers. In a pool of luxurious sunshine near the vineyard wall, I was sitting, one bare brown foot turned, up upon my knee. My big toe functioned excellently as a counterpost for the band of wool and goat hair that I was weaving. Intent upon the sling's completion, I did not hear the priest's wife call as she approached.

"Yeshue! Yeshue!"

Beside me now, she startled me. "What? What's the matter, Mary?"

Her hands stirred about excitedly. "Put away your playthings, child. Someone has come to see you." She stepped aside, permitting me to see another figure, a woman, standing shyly in the shadows of the arbor. I was puzzled.

Mary prompted me with gesture and whisper. "Stand up, Yeshue. Stand up." Slowly, I rose, unable to take my eyes from this curiously compelling stranger.

The woman stepped from the shadow, hesitated, raising her hand temple high to draw back a fold of her dark-blue headpiece, revealing her face.

"Mama!" I shouted. "Mama!"

Her arms opened. "Issa, my Issa!" she cried.

Then words failed us, and running one to the other, we embraced in silent, exultant joy!

There were sugary almond cakes and musty wine as dark as blood at Father Demetrius' house, and over this repast, Khatoun related her own trials of the winter gone: Hilwah was sacked by Turks and trampled to the ground. Only a few Syrians along with Khatoun were able to flee to the foothills, and from there she had endured alone. A sixth sense, an awareness, as it were, of danger threatening her son pressed her onward and made finding him her primal concern. Now she had found him, and safe, and healthy. Her travail had not been in vain.

"And your younger son, Madam," the priest asked gently. "Yeshue's brother . . .?"

A ghost of a smile tensed the curve of her thin lips, as though the question raised the curtain of her mind upon a scene so sad its very distance back in time by contrast sponsored now an odd, pathetic pleasure.

"Malky . . . is with my Soumay now . . . with his father."

Father Demetrius crossed himself. "And with God, good lady."

I was less tactful. "But what happened to him, Mama?" I begged. "What happened to little Malky? How did my brother die?"

Her dark eyes avoiding mine, her gaze wandered to the doorway and outside to the glorious springtime exploding upon the mountains. "During the burning and the shooting," she said soberly, "Malky was separated from me and ran off in terror. Somewhere, another woman trapped inside a building screamed for her own son. A

Turkish soldier—so they told me, for I did not see it— picked him up by his tiny leg, shouted, 'Here is your little Christian lion, woman,' and hurled the baby against the burning wall. . . ."

For a moment there were no sounds except the distant bleating of a protesting goat and the shrill bickerings of birds of morning. Khatoun's face remained impassively still. I felt fear and outrage swelling within my temples. I looked to Father Demetrius, who returned my gaze openly and without comment.

I have told you your position, the priest seemed to be thinking. Hate the war . . . and the savagery . . . . But you must love the man—Christ died for both of you.

I remembered, struggled within my heart to replace my hatred for this nameless unknown Turk with something akin to forgiveness, and found by thinking on the man with pity that I could! And something calm and peaceful was restored to me.

But it was *not* Malky!

With a wild, searing wail, I threw my head into the lap of my mother's robe and cried my heart out.

A few days later, I lay sprawled on my belly in the courtyard, applying the finishing touches to my sling, while my mother's deft fingers conjured from a long cottony fleece lying across her lap like an earthbound cloud a single, sturdy strand of wool. It was late in a golden afternoon, and we had been talking animatedly of the old, happy days in Hilwah. Now for some moments she had been silent, curling the wool round and round the primitive wooden loom. Mary had graciously provided her with new clothing. The strand broke. My mother found another and continued.

"We will be leaving in the morning, Yeshue," she said quietly. I looked up in surprise just as Father Demetrius came into the courtyard.

"And all the women that were wisehearted did spin with their hands," he said warmly.

She smiled. "Who told you that, Father?" she asked.

"Why, Holy Scripture, good woman. Exodus, I believe."

She commenced her spinning. "I hope it is true then, for as I spun I have made a decision."

I scrambled to my feet. "Mama says we must leave tomorrow, Father Demetrius!"

He raised a hand in protest. My mother overlooked it. "You and your good wife, Father, have done so much already," she told him. "We cannot impose upon you any longer."

The young priest called his wife and reported my mother's plan. Mary rushed to her side. "But dear Khatoun," she pleaded. "Where will you go? Hilwah is destroyed and in the mountains between here and Basibrina you would surely be set upon by Kurds. Pray, stay with us in Tour-Abdeen. At least until this terrible war is over."

My mother shook her head. "You are both kind, and true followers of Our Lord, but I am young yet and able to work. It is not right that I should shift to other hands the responsibilities which God has given me."

"But where, Khatoun?" Mary repeated. "Where will you go?"

"To a city. Nisibin first. There I shall find work and provide for Yeshue. That is what my Soumay would have wished me to do."

Still hoping to forestall this rash young woman from her plans, the priest and his wife went into the house.

"Must we *really* go, Mama?" I asked. She nodded her head and traced the edge of my chin with her fingers. "But why, Mama? Why can't we stay here?"

She leaned toward my querulous forehead. "Because I have made a promise," she said as she kissed me. "And it is time to begin its fulfillment."

"A promise," I echoed. "To my father?"

"To God," was her soft reply.

"But what was your promise, Mama? What did you promise God?"

Smiling, she put a finger to her lips. Then she led me into the house, where Mary had lighted the first saucer of oil against the shadows of the falling twilight.

Like everything else sullied with the war's despoiling touch, Nisibin when we arrived there two days later seemed drastically different from the city that I had so happily visited in the years before.

The central bazaar, once a thriving stir of color, gorgeous silks, and gleaming silver embroidery brought by caravan from Damascus, was a gutted ruin—the result of raiding Kurds and Arabs burning and looting in the fore and wake of battle. No merchants met to argue in the once busy coffee gardens—such benches as had not been torn apart for firewood stood empty in disordered nakedness—and the ancient streets, streets that had channeled the carriages of kings, served now to shuttle silent, suspicious people, with pinched and haggard faces, haunted eyes and feeble frames, in their pathetic search for worm-eaten figs and other such commodities as were available at enormous prices for their sustenance.

In the ancient church of St. James of Nisibin we encountered fellow Syrians whose flight had brought them this far into Mesopotamia.

"Yes," they told us. "The British are at Baghdad and have crossed the Sinai Desert—perhaps Palestine will fall to them before the winter. But Syria, from Damascus to Aleppo, is suffering terribly. Not a month ago, King Hussein of Hedjaz took possession of Aqaba. Christians are pressed on every side and dying by the thousands from starvation and disease."

A Lebanese Syrian spoke of his country's plight: "All the old liberties have been abolished. We were an industrious and pacific little nation until Turkey saw her empire begin to totter. Now the Grand Council has been suppressed, and Turkish governors rule despotically in Batron and Zahle."

But from my mother's point of view, these were distant troubles. More urgently, there was the need for work.

"Oh, you shall find work here, Madam," the Syrians told her. "If you don't mind laboring from dawn to dusk for the price of a few olives and a piece of bread, if you're

strong enough to cart heavy rails of iron and lengths of
oaken log, if your soft hands are capable of digging ditches
till the blisters break and bleed, and if your Christian
eyes can bear watching the Armenian prisoners beaten to
death by Turks. Yes, Madam, there is work here in Nisibin.
The Germans are building a magnificent railway. There is
work for everyone — if you can survive it."

My mother pressed her arm around my shoulder. Her
hand was trembling slightly. "We will survive it," she
said with sudden calmness. "God will watch over us."

In the weeks that followed, we saw most of the Syrian's
predictions come true. Before dawn each morning the
Armenians were force-marched from their white-tented
prison camp on the desert side of the tracks to begin a day
whose wretched hours of arduous effort crawled sluggishly
one by one into the weary hunger-ridden night. And side
by side with the Armenians, my mother and other hirelings
worked just as hard — though, fortunately, they were subject only to vicious lashings of the tongue from the Turkish
and German supervisors; the whip and rifle butt were
reserved for the Armenians.

The health and weight that had been restored to me while
with Father Demetrius ebbed away again under the meager
diet supplied by the pitifully small wage my mother earned.
Often, the children of the workers, and I along with them,
would wait beside the refuse piles of the military bivouacs
in hopes of gleaning some small bone or crust or some
kernels of discarded wormy rice, and from those children
I learned to speak Armenian. And though nearly half a
century stands between those days and this, one scene
persists in stinging bitterness as if it had happened yesterday:

Skinny, grimy children were pawing through the garbage near a German mess tent. Their famished fingers
scurried like bony moles among the slops, and shot to their
whimpering, drawn mouths with any morsel that those
fingers found. A few feet away, in crisp, resplendent glory
a tall, burnished German officer watched their miserable

hunt as he fed his sleek stallion succulent mouthfuls of sweet, juicy raisins.

The winter of 1917 was severe in Nisibin. Icy gales and blinding dust storms slowed the progress of the railway considerably. Even the slaves could not work if the weather was too wicked for their masters, and thus many days had to be passed inside the wind-whipped makeshift tents provided by the gracious German employers. And the frozen nights were the source of another terror—one we had never dreamed possible.

Far south, beyond the eastern horizon of the desert, British aircraft carried out sporadic raids in the area of Mosul and fabled, fated Nineveh. Often the deep, dark firmament reflected in angry and ominously silent explosions a preamble to the age of death from the sky which was then awakening.

More and more pertinently, the horrors of the war imposed upon us. Old men and women collapsed in hunger and died uncomforted in the gutters of the street, while shabby, surly Turkish troops, arrogantly indifferent to the hysterical commands of mounted Prussian officers, came and went in increasing chaos. Our pathetic Christmas that year was cheered only by the insistent rumor that Jerusalem, the Holy City, had been wrested from the infidel's hand after six centuries of occupation.

By summer, the British successes along the Tigris and lower Euphrates had halted the southbound roadwork. The Armenians were marched off to what macabre destiny we never knew, and one autumn morning the "free workers" were ordered aboard a fouled and vermin-ridden cattle train to be transported westward toward Ras-El-Ain and Aleppo.

Nearly as tall as my mother now, I swung myself agilely up into the car and, clearing a place among the others squatting there, I reached out and took her hand. The others inside squabbled and bickered over seating space. She would *not* sit in the dusty filth. In spite of her privations her natural dignity had not yet vanished, and though the jour-

ney might be hours, even days, I resolved to stand proudly
beside her. I thought of her as she had been in Hilwah—
quick as a bird and beautiful to look upon. Even last year
in the mountains of Tour-Abdeen, she was a young woman
with her health, her quiet grace, her youth within her.
Now, she had aged perceptibly. Her once bright eyes
gazed from dark and sunken sockets; her hands had become
stiff and coarse with menial toil. Soumay would not have
recognized her as his wife. It was a harsh heaven, I thought,
to take so much from this good woman.

"It cannot be worse, Issa," she whispered. "It may
even be better."

"What, Mama?"

"You seem pensive. I said it might be better where
we're going."

"Oh, I wasn't thinking about that, Mama."

"Then why are you so sad?"

"It's nothing. I'm not sad. I was—"

"Yes?"

"I—I was trying to read, Mama. See what someone has
scratched here on the wooden side of the car."

A bearded old man shuffled beside us, juggling dirty
packages wrapped in shredded newsprint. "How could
you read that, boy?" he grunted intrusively.

The woman stiffened. "He *can* read some words. And
each day he learns more."

The old man grinned, fetid breath puffing from a tobacco-
stained mouth. "If you are Syrians, as I think you are—
being no fool, then I say he can't read a word of that. It is
Armenian if you must know and being, as I said, no fool
and once a scholar, I do not make mistakes."

Testy or not, it was refreshing to find a learned, out-
spoken man among this sullen and moribund group of
travelers. "Then, would you read it, sir?" I inquired.

The old man sniffed as if he scented a mockery, then
leaning forward, he squinted watery, red-veined eyes and
cleared his throat. "Our dwelling," he read, "is on the
mountains. We have no longer any need of a roof to cover

us; we have already drained the bitter cup of death; we have no more need of a judge."

With the screech of iron, the scream of steam, and the battering of wooden cars, the wretched train began to move. The old man stumbled past them, grumbling his way through the closely jammed human herd. To what fate, I wondered, had this train delivered the Armenian who had inscribed these despairing words? I placed my arm around my mother's waist to steady her. *We have already drained the bitter cup of death.* Perhaps we *had* been protected. "You are right, Mama," I told her thoughtfully. "It will be better. God will see to it."

And, with the redoubtable assistance of the British Army, He assuredly did.

A few miles past Ras-El-Ain, the train scraped and squealed to a jarring halt. The day had begun as a warm one, but a chilling wind swept now across the desert, hissing sand through the cattle-car slats. With patience born of long-suffering, the passengers pulled lengths of torn turbans and soiled shawls across their faces and stoically waited for the train to move again. For perhaps an hour we waited in this fashion until at last the wind was spent and a progressively hotter sun beat down upon the wooden roof. The rusty water bucket had long been empty. Toilet facilities were nonexistent. We could see only sand and sky to the south and to the north only the green teeth of distant mountains. The cars before us and behind us, of course, shared our circumstances, but the walls between were solid and we could not see our fellow sufferers. As noon approached, the people grew more vocal in their discontent. Some began banging protests on the wooden slats; women in another car could be heard wailing. The stench of sweating, long-unbathed bodies became unbearable.

From the track side where the German-Turkish mounted escort had been patrolling there was a forbidding silence. No soldier had been seen for quite some time.

Then, from a few cars toward the front, a shout went up. It was alarming in its excitation but it had an apparent impetus of joy. The wave of hurrahs came closer. A moment later the car directly ahead of us shared in its contagion. Madness had at last claimed all our brothers, we thought, until a wind-burned, grinning Bedouin reined up a sweat-foamed mount beside our own car and breathlessly shouted his news.

"The Franks and Turks have fled!" he called in a patois of Syrian and Arabic. "The English he is now win all Aleppo. Someone soon will come to move your train of sadness-no-longer."

The English had taken Aleppo! For months that ancient city had been the greatest boast of the German-Turkish Alliance. Though Allenby's forces had redeemed Jerusalem and the troops of General Marshall were breathing hot on Mosul, Aleppo it was said, Aleppo, high on its fertile oasian hillocks, with forces powerfully concentrated under Field Marshal Machensen, Aleppo was impregnable. Yet the Union Jack flew over it this afternoon! With the new-born energy of freedom, the passengers forced the sides of the cars and leaped wildly to the railroad bed. And the *unconquerable* Turks and Germans who had been our masters and escorts were now only distant skeins of desert dust rising in the sun between ourselves and the Turkish mountains.

It was Saturday, October 26, 1918. British cavalry and armored cars had entered Aleppo early that morning, cutting off traffic on the Constantinople-Baghdad Railway as they did. This railway, upon a section of which our very train had been stalled in the afternoon heat, had been the artery of supply for the Turkish forces opposing General Marshall on the Tigris and Euphrates. Three days later, after a long, stubborn fight on the reeded banks of the Tigris, his troops defeated the Turks and severed their last communications with Mosul. The main objectives of both the Palestinian and Mesopotamian campaigns had been achieved; the remaining Turkish forces were checkmated.

On October 31, Turkey laid down her arms and signed an

armistice that was tantamount to unconditional surrender. The Ottoman Empire was reduced to a shadow of its former self, and history muffled at last the brutal thunder that had echoed across Asia Minor and the Christian world since a day four hundred and sixty-five years before when Mohammed II vengefully spurred his horse into the Cathedral of St. Sophia.

Many of the train's passengers gathered in front of the halted engine and, raising their voices in a raucous chorus of hymn and hollering, optimistically prepared to walk the remaining hundred miles to Aleppo.

My mother and I were among the last to leave the cattle car, and when I bolted down and turned to help her follow, I saw the two shabby packages that the wise old man had apparently discarded or forgotten in his newfound taste of freedom. Somewhere in the exuberant, assembling crowds, he was singing at the top of his voice. I did not recognize the song. I had never heard "God Save the King" before.

Aleppo, old City of the Citadel, might as well have been Babel for all the myriad tongues and customs, uniforms and nationalities, assembled there. Refugees, and former conscripts from the Turkish forces—many deserters, many horribly maimed—in addition to unsettled nomads separated from their tribes, all roamed the streets and spelled potential trouble. The British, however, with their traditional esteem for order, lost no time in regulating this milieu. Centuries-old streets and alleys never before illuminated at night except by the moon were made bright with electricity. A local police force was raised under military guidance. Hospitals were reestablished and a fire brigade formed. Courts of civil justice were set up and the elimination of oppressive taxes declared immediately. Guarantees were made with neighboring sheikhs, and the sheikhs in turn were held responsible for the conduct of their tribesmen. Justice, of course, was often summary, with variable but effective sentences. A public servant found stealing government property, for example, might be ordered to carry through the bazaar such an inscription as "With this hand I receive from the government," held high in one hand and another, "With this hand, I steal from the government," in the other hand.

As each month passed, the pleasanter aspects of living began to rekindle the spirit of the city. The fruit crops were poor that season, but the bazaars blossomed again to life.

Leather goods, bright silks and cottons, wool carpets in vivid intricate patterns, shone from the stalls in the sunlight, and the onlooker's eye, too long inured by the clouded drabness of the war, was stunned by this hypnotic feast of color.

Tirelessly, the Red Cross tried to house and feed the hungry, homeless thousands, and British soldiers provided great barrels of food from which the children could be assured ample and nutritious portions.

Word reached us in the spring that since a French mandate had been declared over much of southern Turkey, it was not difficult to get work there for at least subsistent wages; so traveling northeast over those same rails by which the Germans had hoped to conquer and control all Asia Minor, we reached Adana, the capitol of the Seyhan Province on the river of the same name.

Originally colonized by the Romans, Adana had prospered since the days of Haroun-al-Rashid and despite the ravages of the war she still maintained herself a bristling center of commerce, industry, and agriculture. We stopped on our way to Adana in a village called Dort-Youl which meant in Turkish, the Four Roads. Four roads were about all there was to this sleepy hamlet but those roads passed through some of the richest orange groves in the world and though we knew nothing then of the wonders of vitamin C, a natural instinct told us that in addition to work and wages the available fresh fruit that we were permitted to eat to our hearts' content would revitalize both body and spirit.

Invigorated by a sweetness in the air that I had never

before tasted, I climbed monkeywise higher and higher up through the comfortable limbs of the tree, careful to stay near the trunk so as not to dislodge wastefully the fat ripe fruits weighing down the end of every branch.

"You will fall, Yeshue," a companion called.

"No, I won't. I will climb to the very top. Watch me, if you are afraid to come."

"I'm not afraid."

"Then come on."

Higher and higher, this way and that, we wound through the branches. "See, I told you I would reach the top."

"All right. We've done it. Now let us go down before we fall. Please."

"Wait. Let me look. I've never been so high. There! Over there! That little white tower is in Dort-Youl and you can see—we must be able to—ahh!"

"What? What is it, Yeshue?"

I was speechless. To the south, now that I had swung around, I could see the last reaches of the orange groves and beyond—and what was beyond was dizzying in its beauty. As far as the horizon, as flat as the desert, in magnificent undulations of every shade of blue and sapphire, azure and indigo, the Queen of the Seas, the Mediterranean, glistened and glittered in the morning sun. For a child of the desert, the mountains, the plain, it was a scene that halted the heart. I climbed down slowly, reluctantly, eyes wide—afraid in blinking them that I might erase the wonder they had just beheld.

Reaching the ground I turned to see my mother hurrying toward me. If she had come to scold me for being so high, it did not matter; the sight was worth the scolding. But she was smiling, talking excitedly. She had news, good news, and in a moment she was all but pulling me after her in the direction of our quarters. There was talk of bathing—in the middle of the day!—and of a journey that must be made at once.

I came to a stop. "Wait, Mama. I didn't understand you. What about Adana? What about the French?"

"There is a school now, Issa. A real and proper school. The French have opened it in Adana. All Syrian children will be going there. A friend has told me only this morning. And we must go at once to Adana to be sure there is room for you."

So the sea and the tall accomodating trees must wait for another time. By evening, we had arrived by train at Adana, and I had been introduced to Father Mansour Tannourji and Mr. John Haroun, the administrator of the school, and they had accepted me into their care.

As the days spun by, charged with the excitement of young minds offered their initial formal challenges, my shyness waned and for the first time in many years I could speak of others easily and truly as my friends.

There was young Boulos Gelph, a sensitive, introspective boy, and the Sowmy brothers—the gentler Abraham, the often reckless Butros—who had also found a camaraderie with me. Butros, his eyes gleaming like black pearls, and the constant grimace on his dark, skinny face could goad even older, stronger boys into cocky battle. More often than not, Butros set up the fights for others as a trainer spurs a camel in his heat into the jealous circle of his foe. Then Butros stood aside and watched, gleefully jabbing his admiring brother in the ribs. Boulos Gelph had warned me in the first days to beware this rash youth and his intrigues but somewhere along the way, as happens in the courts of boyhood, a silent pact was made between us and a curious friendship sparkled from it.

From Butros' point of view it might have been public relations, so to speak, for in the institution, I was a celebrity of sorts. As a stranger among them the other children pointed and whispered as I passed, for a rumor of almost mythical priority preceded me: in this world of orphans, of children of the war, I had something the others had only heard of, prayed for, or dreamed about. "That is he," they whispered. "That is the one. His name is Yeshue. He has a real, live mother."

There were perhaps two hundred children in the orphanage at Adana and dedicated teachers such as Hanna Shami, Paul John, and Ibrahim Hagwerdi did their utmost to instill in each of us the rudiments of French and Arabic and our ancient native language, Syriac. They were good men all, bringing order and education to youngsters whose lives and families had suffered the wars disintegration.

It was also here that I first met the beloved Father Hanna Dolabani, a thin, saintly man whose simple manner and quiet humility rarely bespoke his keen mind and erudition. It was from Father Dolabani, through his classroom lectures, his moving homilies, and our treasured walks together that the real seeds of my faith began to thrive.

True, I had fortunately never lacked for good and godly guidance. From infancy on, God had been for me a demonstrable, beautiful fact deeply woven into the warp and woof of my life. But now, an adolescent, I was more appreciative and my imagination more sharply spurred. Once it had seemed that the Syrian Church of Antioch was simply the one to which I, by politics and geography, belonged, as the Bedouins and the Kurds were Muslim Sunnites, but when her noble history and her holy rites were made clear to me, a new fire kindled from the ashes of my boyhood complacency, and I began to view my faith and church as enviable treasures not to be taken for granted, never to be betrayed or given up.

From the past, great names arose to vivify my dreams. Our Blessed Lord, of course, first throughout eternity, and then Saint Peter, establishing in A.D. 37 the Church of Antioch which, though the city itself was Greek, held all rituals and orders in Syriac. And thus it is that the name of Antioch lawfully applies to the Syrian Church. Alexandria, Constantinople, Rome would follow, but Saint Peter had acted first in Antioch, and Christians, under *that* name, were prospering there before The Gospel According to John was put to parchment. Her great saints and martyrs, her builders and rebuilders, her apologists and interpreters, her saints: Ignatius, John Chrysostom, Severius, Philoxenus of Mabbogh, Jacob, Ephrem, Ahodama, James of Sarugh, Cyril of Alexandria, Bar-Hebraeus, Patriarch Michael the Great; protectors such as Empress Theodora and even her brutal prosecutors: Anusharwan, Emperor Justinian—these were the names and the histories that enthralled me. I could not learn about them quickly enough.

The months added up to a year, then swallowed the half of another, and though my mother, looking up from her polishing or putting aside the laundry, wished aloud that I would fatten my frame by devouring bread and *burghul* as I then devoured books, it was for us again a happy time.

But on May 11, 1920, halfway around the world, the proper dignitaries were adding their signatures to a paper in the Clock Room of the French Foreign Office at Versailles. This pact, after administrative assistance by a mandate government would recognize Syria and Mesopotamia as independent states. It would also return Adana to the humbled, potentially vengeful Turks; the orphanage would have to be vacated!

Father Dolabani was the only one who faced this development with unshaken faith.

"Why then, if we must move, we will move," he said simply.

The children, woefully acquainted with the wretchedness of being shuffled from place to place, crowded about him like fretting chicks beneath a mother hen. "But how will we do it?" "There are so many of us. Where will we go?"

Father Dolabani stroked his beard.

"Far across the sea," he told us, "there is a great land where everyone is healthy and happy and free. It is almost a magic land in some ways, because not very long ago, as *we* reckon history, it didn't even exist."

The children responded excitedly. "Will we go there, Father?" they cried. "Is that where we will go?" "And there are no Turks in such a wondrous land, are there, Father?"

He raised a hand to calm them. "Wait. Wait. Wait. One at a time."

"No. We shall not go there because it is very, very far away. There are Turks there too, I'm sure, though not such Turks as you have learned to fear. All people are there. That is the wonder of it. All people from all lands live together and are happy. And tonight I shall write letters to many of our countrymen who have gone there to seek their fortunes and they will send us money to find a new home for every one of you."

The children cheered in delighted relief. Only one youngster's curiosity had not been fully satisfied. "Father Hanna," he asked. "What is the name of that country?"

"It is called America," the priest replied. "And many people call it the hope of the world."

Father Dolabani's faith in his American friends was justified; their contributions and support allowed him to open another institution in the friendlier clime of Lebanon, in the city of Beirut, but a short while before the French authorities transferred the children, my mother advised me of her own plans for my future.

"But, Mama," I protested. "All my friends are here: Father Hanna and Boulos Gelph and the Sowmy brothers. Can we not wait and leave with them for Beirut?"

She shook her head. "It is time for us to go, Yeshue. I have saved a little money and can take care of you. The new orphanage will have more children than room, and it wouldn't be fair if you took a place another boy might need desperately — a boy without mother or father or anyone."

There was no denying the justice of her stand, but it did not immediately ease the heaviness of my heart. "But where will we go, Mama?"

"Do you remember, Yeshue, what I told you that evening in Tour-Abdeen?"

"At Father Demetrius' house?"

She nodded. I could see the twilight falling on the little courtyard, smell again the blossoms of the olive trees—before the slavery of Nisibin, the hungers of Aleppo, before the sunshine of Dort-Youl and the joys of school life here in Adana. Had so much passed between? Had so much gone before? And I recalled what she had told me.

"You said you ... made a promise, Mama."

Again, she nodded. "In those dark days when I was in Hilwah. Your father, your brother dead, only a small chance that I would ever see you alive. In the depths of that misery, I made a promise."

"To God, you told me."

"Yes. To God. I promised him that if I found you alive and he spared us through the war that we would go as pilgrims to the holy places where he lived when he was on this earth. We began that pilgrimage when we left Tour-Abdeen. Now it is time to continue."

"To Bethlehem, Mama. Will we see the stable there?"

"To Jerusalem first. To the Holy Sepulcher."

We left by boat a few days later, and the glorious adventure of setting forth on the Mediterranean if only for so brief a voyage did much to diminish my remorse at parting. The green hills of the Turkish border sank behind us, and, far to the west, the merest tip of Cyprus broke the sea. Southward, we sailed through waters Saint Paul had navigated, past promontories that had first beheld the masts and sails of the crusaders' avenging warships. At Latakia, we paused to discharge and take on passengers and then too soon, too soon, the bolder headlands hedged us in and we docked at Tripoli—which was as far as our funds could carry us.

Acting on the advice of friends, we traveled inland to the city of Homs in Syria. There, as we had been told, we found many fellow Syrians, homeless refugees mostly, urgently anxious to find work, to start mending if possible the disruptions the war had brought to their lives.

There were people there willing to help even if it meant personal sacrifices; my mother soon had work and I was again placed in a school. Within a few months, however, the situation in Homs became very uncomfortable for all refugees such as us. Feeling perhaps that too large a charitable output was endangering the financial security of his own jurisdiction, no less a personage than the Archbishop made it known that transient Syrians were not welcome within the city. It seemed a curiously unkind edict to issue from so high a Christian office, but each man must make the decisions befitting his rank and be prepared ultimately to be judged by Almighty God for their intrinsic values. In any case, we were no longer welcomed in Homs.

With others in the same plight, we wandered from town to town, finding some work in this village, some charity in that, and at last we reached Damascus which, despite our continued privations, was an awesome place for a youth whose religion was becoming more and more paramount in his life.

The oldest continuously inhabited city in the world, Damascus existed two thousand years before the coming of Christ. It is among the most beautiful and historically romantic cities ever known, with a five-mile wall that has weathered the centuries, its seven gates still standing as solidly as they did in A.D. 1148 under the vain onslaught of the Crusaders. It is said that the description of Paradise in the Koran is taken from the city, and for generations the Arabs have called it the Pearl of the Desert.

"You can sup or breakfast in Damascus for nothing," an old traveler will tell you, and for much of the year, when the gentle Abana flowing through the heart of the city makes of it an oasis of fertile glory, this is very nearly true. But even if one *is* hungry now and again in the city, Damascus offers many consolations. The "Street called Straight," as the main thoroughfare in known, is the very place where Saint Paul dwelt after his conversion to the faith of Christ. Amawi Mosque rises above the site of a church constructed by the Empress Helena. One can walk there assured that there are more desperate hungers than the stomach knows and that the Lord God has provided food for even these.

From Damascus, we crossed the Anti-Lebanon mountains and reached the Mediterranean coast again at Beirut. There I had a chance to renew my friendship again at the orphanage but this time I was not nearly so loathe to leave, for our journeying had brought us to edges of the Holy Land and we could not travel a day southward now without myriad encounters with the realities of the Testaments.

Past the once-accursed cities of Tyre and Sidon, we journeyed into the marshland surrounding Lake Hulah. Here, Bedouin women, barefoot in the mud, harvested the long-stemmed papyrus, the bulrushes of the Bible. Bundles would be taken to their homes and the reeds woven into tents and mats just as the mother of Moses wove her protective "ark." Southward a few miles to the ruins of Hazor, a Canaanite city destroyed by Joshua more than three thousand years ago, and on to Capernaum nesting on the edge of the somberly beautiful Sea of Galilee, where thunderous storms rush down from the surrounding mountains. Here Jesus "rebuked the winds . . .; and there was a great calm." Past Endor, whose prophesying witch predicted the deaths of Saul and his sons in the battle of Gilboa; through sleepy, crumbling Nain, where Jesus raised to life the widow's only son; and thence across the Plains of Esdraelon, the grassy corridor through the rocky hills of lower Galilee wherein have echoed the clashes of battle since Deborah sat under her oak. Then through the fertile hills and valleys of Samaria, along the incredible trough of the Jordan valley, past the reed-thatched hovels of a worn and weary Jericho and at last, fittingly in Holy Week, we reached Jerusalem.

Jerusalem! Women in heavy white linen dresses and long beaded veils weighed down with silk embroidery of scarlet, orange, green, and gold; blind beggars, and some not so blind, singing of their plight to the passerby; the fez-shaped tarbooshes of busy men bobbing like bright red corks upon a sea of veils and hatless heads, and, above the noisy crowds, the exotic, lilting strains of a zamoora ribboning from one of the gabled windows projecting out over the narrow, cobbled streets.

Countrywomen were hawking cauliflowers, artichokes, cucumbers, and fat silken tomatoes. A querulous water vendor argued the price of pungent meat chunks roasting on iron spits over a tiny charcoal fire. Well-fed tourists, with cameras slung over their shoulders, moved more shyly among the bustling natives, persistently assaulted by the sellers of souvenirs. There was the tinsel-white beard of a scurrying rabbi, the scarlet plumage of a Roman monsignor, the ornate flowing cape of an orthodox patriarch — and hovering over everything, like some intoxicating cloud, the incense breathed from the doors and windows of hundreds of churches.

Fifteen years old now and taller than my mother, I guided her through the crowds toward the Church of the Holy Sepulcher. I moved in stunned, hypnotic awe and expected at any moment to see the multitude parting so that a gentle man upon a timorous donkey might pass as children shouted: *Hosanna, Son of David. Blessed art Thou who comest in the name of the Lord.*

We had reached Jerusalem. The promise had been kept.

BOOK
TWO

Show me thy ways, O Lord;
Teach me thy paths.
Lead me in thy truth, and teach me:
For thou art the God of my salvation;
On thee do I wait all the day.
Remember, O Lord, thy tender mercies and
    thy loving-kindnesses;
For they have been ever of old.
Remember not the sins of my youth.

—From the Twenty-fifth Psalm

ALREADY THE FIRST RAYS OF DAWN COLORED THE MIN-
aret shaft of the Tower of David with the cool pink blush
of new-cut melons. The monastery had been up and astir
for some hours now, but soon the whole of Jerusalem would
know the bustle of a busy Monday morning.

"I wish he would hurry," a young man said aloud,
and the tonsured old monk in charge of the refectory reminded him that impatience was bad for the digestion.

This wise advice notwithstanding, we washed down
bread, eggs, and fruit with great gulps of fresh milk, eyes
darting constantly toward the refectory door, wishing the
arrival of Father Yacub Salahy.

"He practically said we had permission," another student
remarked reassuringly. "Beyond that, we need only the
approval of the Metropolitan."

The old monk refilled our saucers. "You'll get it. Don't
be worried."

I offered thanksgiving privately and excused myself
from the table. From the refectory window, I could see
groups of early arisen tourists who thoughtfully antici-
pated the mass exodus of fellow travelers from the Holy
City now that Easter Sunday was a day behind. I, too, that
morning, shared the anxiety of my companions for the
adventure and diversion of a trip outside the monastery
walls, but my thoughts also dwelt upon the two full happy
years that had passed since my mother and I had first
arrived in this wondrous place.

Ancient inscription in Aramaic in the Church of St. Mark in Jerusalem. Translation: This is the house of Mary, mother of John, called Mark. Proclaimed a church by the holy apostles under the name of Virgin Mary, mother of God, after the ascension of our Lord Jesus Christ into heaven. Renewed after the destruction of Jerusalem by Titus in the year A.D. 73

The Monastery of St. Mark, sometimes called the Monastery of the Syrians, served also as a parish church and a school for young men. It stood just inside that section of Jerusalem known as the Armenian Quarter, and even a youth too callous to be humbled by the peace and holiness of its monks and priests could not fail to be overwhelmed by the hallowed atmosphere with which the ancient legends and traditions permeated every corridor and corner of the imposing structure: Mary, the mother of John who was called Mark, had once lived here, and it was on this site that the apostles were assembled when Peter entered to inform them that an angel had loosened his bonds and opened the door of the prison. Here, too, tradition firmly maintained, Jesus selected an upper room in which to partake of the Passover with his disciples. In that same room the Holy Spirit one day descended to touch the tongues of those brave men with the diversity of languages.

Even presuming those actual walls and ceilings had long since crumbled to a sacred dust, the present buildings also had a history centuries old. Here ascetics and monks had been housed as early as 1472, long after Syrians in Jerusalem had lost their properties to tyrants and oppressors, and when the Bishop of the Monastery at Magdalene was forced to flee, he sought refuge here and brought with him manuscripts that had been treasured as ancient in the eleventh century.

By now the redder sun edged the crenellations of the citadel, once the impregnable palace of King Herod, and the cries of tradesmen, souvenir sellers, began to give audible proof that the day was well begun. Most of the boys had left the refectory for the early morning duties. In the courtyard below, I could see small clouds of dust rising from the edges of vigorously harassed brooms. Other students, who were taking a holiday, had already passed through the main gate; they were off to visit with families or relatives who lived nearby. Only a dozen of us waited now for Father Salahy.

We twelve were more or less a selected group which luckily my studies at Adana had prepared me for. Day and night we were solicitously watched over and trained by the patient monks and by Father Salahy, our especial patron, who was the spiritual head of the school and our own instructor in the lives of the saints and the teachings of early church fathers. That was why we had sought his aid in our somewhat impetuous plans for spending our Easter vacation.

Michael, a fellow student, approached and stood by me, taking in the morning. He was a gauntly handsome boy with soulful ebony eyes and starkly carved features, and although he was very close to my own age, he seemed already to have attained that tranquillity which is the promise of the contemplative life—though his attitude as often as not could also be interpreted as some painful preoccupation, as if a silent, torturous fire raged within him. Behind us, the others shuffled their sandals on the stone floor impatiently.

"Why are you smiling, Michael?" I asked him.

His dark eyes settled on me softly. "I am thinking of all the more colorful phrases they would be using if they didn't happen to be in a monastery."

I listened a moment, then smiled with him because, light-headed at the thought of a journey after months of books and classrooms, they were indeed struggling to keep their language appropriate to their state.

"Do you think we will get to go?" I asked him.

He shrugged his thin shoulders and cocked his head. "If it is the will of God," he said simply.

Father Salahy's familiar snappy walk brought us as a body to the doorway even before he entered. He was smiling brightly and held up a promising paper sealed with an impressive stamp.

"Here it is, young wanderers," he said. "Your official permission. Bishop Gregorius sends his blessings on your journey and the gracious Greek Patriarch sends instructions to his monks to see that you are well cared for."

We thanked him profusely and bobbed with almost sacrilegious speed for his blessing before we bolted for the corridor.

"And remember," the laughing priest called after us, "We shall have reports on each and every one of you; remember that you represent St. Mark's."

The church bells of Jerusalem were sounding their call to morning worship when we set out into the streets of the city with sandals on our feet, staves in our hands, and bread in our sachels, like the apostles of old. We were bound for the Greek Orthodox Monastery of St. Saba some thirteen miles away, and outside Jerusalem the morning sun glistened across the flowered fields and through the pungent olive groves, and the sparrows twittered their hosannas while we sang matins as we walked. The walk took us along the rocky, winding brink of the gorge of the Kidron, which grew ever wilder as we pursued it. Part of the way we followed the ruins of an old Roman road.

Our communal step was a little less spirited when we reached St. Saba's some six hours later. In youthful overestimation of our capacities, we had hoped to arrive in time for lunch but did not make it. The Abbot, after reading his Patriarch's introduction, welcomed us warmly and assured us that there would be a fine meal waiting after a brief tour of the monastery. The less stouthearted among us might have wished for the nourishment first, for after our tour of the many buildings, built and rebuilt often since the priory was first settled in A.D. 486, we were granted a visit to a bizarre testimonial of early Christian fortitude—a chalky pyramid made up of hundreds and hundreds of crumbling human skulls, martyrs from Persian slaughters of the early seventh century.

At sundown, we went readily to bed, physically weary but exhilarated by the sanctity and fraternity of this ancient community. At two in the morning, we arose with our Greek brethren for divine services and matins, which lasted until well after dawn. For those who were considering the monastic life, it was an early test of stamina and endurance.

Breakfast finished, it was with reluctance that we took up our staffs and prepared to return to Jerusalem. Outside the walls of St. Saba's, however, a heady sense of adventures yet to come seized upon us and impetuously we implored the youth in charge to allow us to make a considerable detour northward along the banks of the Jordan that we might visit another Greek monastery there dedicated to Saint John the Baptist. At first, he was unwilling to exceed the Bishop's instructions but we persisted: the day was bright, the month was April, and we were young. We turned our faces eastward and headed into the desert toward the Dead Sea.

No one dared say it aloud, but we were not long out upon

the gleaming sand when each of us began to doubt the wisdom of our escapade. It was not midmorning yet and our cassocks were soaked with perspiration. Nor did it help our spirits to encounter a wandering Bedouin who shouted, "Where do you think you are going in this wilderness?" And when we told him, he grinned as though we had answered: "To the moon!"

"This is a desolate, dangerous road for fellaheen," he warned us. "There are wolves and other wild beasts — besides the sun. Return to your cool church; leave the desert to the scorpions."

But of course there is no surer way to convince any young man that he *must* do something than by telling him in the presence of other young men that he had probably best not do it. With perspiring heads held high, we ignored him and went on.

Nearing the Dead Sea, the desert gave way to a barrier of crags and rocky piles as grotesque as any Dante could envision. The heat continued oppressively, and the stygian air became thick with the scent of sulphur.

With some newfound enthusiasm, most of the students bounded like young goats among the strange formations of grayish marl, rock salt, and sandstone, arguing humorously over which of them had found Lot's salted wife, for here erosion, wind, and rain had constructed many a promontory image in twisted, humanoid form.

I climbed alongside Michael, who seemed much more fatigued than the others, trying to cheer him up with bantering conversation.

"Did you hear the monk last night telling us about the sounds that come from the skulls at Mar Saba?" I asked him.

"He was joking surely," he replied with a weak smile.

We climbed higher and at last, hundreds of feet below, stretched out before us the Dead Sea surrounded by barren, wasted shore — four hundred square miles of deceptively beautiful water, a sparkling translucent blue, uninhabited by any living fish and seldom trespassed upon by the birds of the air—a fit setting for the lost cities of Sodom and Gomorrah.

"When Abraham and Lot stood here," one student reminded us, "they beheld all the plain and compared it to the Garden of the Lord. Now look at it."

Michael took my arm. "All things are passing," he quoted softly.

Below, we could see along the shores a few naked, sundarkened natives collecting small white pyramids of salt from lagoons in the briny marshes; along the water's edge the slow waves washed up debris fat with the bodies of dead fish that had entered from the River Jordan.

It was nearing noon now and the temperature was all but unbearable; one of the students familiar with the area suggested that we continue just a little farther before finding shadowed spots and waiting out the noonday. "Not far from here, my friends," he said, "there is a spring. It's brackish, but still drinkable. As I remember, it is only a mile or so north. The Bedouins call it Ain Feshkha."

"Ain Feshkha?"

"Yes. *A Step*. Come along. We shall at least have water with our bread."

Brackish or not, the anticipation of water was great. We started out following him. Only Michael wavered. I returned to him and put out my hand.

"Come. He says it is not far."

He was breathing heavily, and the perspiration ran like rain across his drawn, dark cheeks.

"I'll try," he said, "but I don't think . . ." and before the sentence was finished, he had fainted.

He revived within minutes but was obviously without strength. We took turns carrying him to Ain Feshkha, where we made him drink of the strangely flavored water, and bathed his face and feet. Then each of us followed suit and having eaten and refreshed ourselves, tried to decide what to do next.

"It is impossible to retrace our steps," our leader told us. "Someone must go and hire a donkey for Michael if there are any to be found."

The student who had led us to Ain Feshkha again supplied the answer.

"Yeshue," he said. "Come with me. Kalia is a few miles
north. There are workers there and where there are workers,
there are always donkeys."

I agreed to accompany my well-informed classmate.

"What are working men doing out in this wasteland?" I
asked as we started off.

"Building," he answered. "They are building a plant
to take potash and bromine from the waters."

I nodded toward the sea. "From *those* waters?" I asked.

He slapped my shoulder teasingly. "You should read
more chemistry and less theology, Yeshue," he said with
a laugh. "The Dead Sea is full of minerals."

"And when do *you* find time to learn all this chemistry?" I inquired.

"Oh, I don't read it, either," he confessed. "My uncle
works for the Palestine Potash Company."

We walked on toward Kalia, and in the discomforting
heat we did not waste more energy in talk, but time by time
I found myself looking out over that broad body of water
with a new respect. Could it be that out of that brine-sodden
morass man might derive elements that would restore
these shores to their ancient luxuriance? I prayed it might
be so, but not without recalling the baleful prediction of
Ezekiel, who withheld from this doomed region the
general "healing" that would come to Palestine, relegating
"the marshes thereof [to be] given up to salt."

There were workmen indeed at Kalia, for the springs
there luckily afforded them in that dire heat water for both
drinking and bathing, whereas the Dead Sea, bitter to the
taste and oily to the touch, could be used for neither. We
hired a donkey and sent it back for Michael. Then, taking
advantage of the delay, we bathed and took a well-earned
rest.

Late into the evening, our reassembled party at last
reached St. John's Monastery on the wild, rocky slopes

of the valley just north of the spot where the Jordan spills into the Dead Sea. The monastery was small and unpretentious, with only a handful of monks to attend it and most of them very, very old. But they were hospitable and gracious nonetheless. We dined well and were warmly encouraged to spend the night, and, having the assurance of their age and wisdom that our Bishop would understand, we were easily convinced.

On a limestone balcony badly in need of repair, I stood alone. Inside, the others rested or offered news and gossip of the city to the aging monks. Out here, the night was falling on this most sacred of waters. The Jordan, the Descender, was in broad flood now with springtime; the full moon's dappled reflection was a murky red in the muddy waters.

Looking down toward the moribund expanse of the Sea of Salt, it was difficult to believe that only sixty miles north the Jordan began in the tranquil Sea of Galilee beneath Mt. Hermon's radiant snows and more difficult to realize that it took this river a twisting course three times as long to make its journey, mostly through a narrow valley fissured ages past when the crust of the earth erupted under incredible prehistoric pressures. Beginning in free-flowing beauty, it ended ugly and unnavigable in a wretched swamp whose waters released themselves only to the sun. Yet, imbued in every mile of it was some manifestation of God's patient plan for his straying children, some mystical reality that is the source of hope for all pathetic human aspirations.

These were the waters which parted that the Ark of the Covenant might pass; these were the shores on which Naaman the Syrian was cured of his leprosy. And somewhere here where these same streams and rivulets converge, He who with a word could *dry* all rivers stood humbly to be baptised at the hands of John and the Father spoke from the heavens and the Dove was seen to descend — and the world of man first received the revelation of the Three who were One.

"Repent! For the Kingdom of Heaven is at hand!"

Startled, I whirled about. A jaunty little monk, smile beaming above his gray beard, came quickly across to the balistrade.

"That's what old John told them down there by the river. And some of them listened and some of them didn't."

"I was thinking about him, Brother," I confessed.

"So I thought when I saw you standing out here studying the Jordan."

"It must be good to spend your life . . . so close to such a holy place."

"Yes. And better still if there were more willing to do it."

"More, Brother?"

"More monks, my son. There should be others here. I suppose you've noticed that my brothers and I are not spring lambs."

"I did, Brother."

"It's you boys. You boys should be thinking about it. Who will be here when we go?"

"But we—that is—we are Syrians, Brother."

"I know that. I didn't mean in *this* monastery. But out here. Here in Saint John's wilderness. Here where he prepared the way of the Lord. Build your own. But it must be kept, the vigil must be kept. Who knows when God again will use these rocks, these waters, these plains for his sacred purposes? Someone must keep the vigil of the wilderness, must make the paths straight in the desert. Someone."

There was deep silence now as the monk turned away. Only the Jordan whispered silkily, and down near the water's edge among the cane and tamarisk, willow and acacia, covering riverbanks where lion and leopard once lurked, some small night creature scurried.

His worn and veined hands traced the balistrade's edge. "Am I an old man spouting nonsense, boy," he asked quietly, "or do I make sense to you in what I said?"

"Much sense, good Brother," I replied. "Much sense, indeed."

"Then think on it. And tell the others. And pray for us."
His hands were swallowed in the long folds of his sleeves.
He turned back toward the monastery. "And now I must
go in. The morning bell seems to ring earlier every day."

"Brother—one thing?"

He yawned. He would be done with talk. "Yes?"

"When John was announcing the Coming, and the Kingdom of Heaven at hand—I mean—out *here*—well, who
was there to hear him—out here?"

The old monk thought for a long moment, then shook
his head. "I don't know," he answered with another yawn.
"But somebody was. Even then, somebody was keeping
the vigil here in the wilderness."

Having had our day in the desert sun, we learned from
our experience and the following morning we set out in
the direction of Jericho long before the first light of dawn
troubled the dark horizon.

Jericho! Surrounded by solid walls six thousand years
before the birth of Christ. Solid walls, until the Lord took
sides with Joshua, and after seven days of circling the city,
the shouts went up, the horns blared forth their threat, and
the walls crumbled like so much papier-mâché.

No wonder, when in midmorning we entered the sleepy
remnants of that once great city, we imagined ourselves
invading Israelites, with orders to spare only the harlot
Rahab and her household, and to add the gold and silver
to the treasures of the Lord! But our fantasy was shattered
as we passed the post office, for a shouting official emerged
from there threateningly waving a telegram.

Our Bishop was worried for our safety and had inquired
after us in this manner, and a worried bishop, it seemed,
made for a flustered postmaster. He wasted no words in
encouraging us to return to Jerusalem.

We acted quickly upon his suggestion but we had hardly
left the city limits when our mischievous sense of freedom
again took hold and we decided that inasmuch as it was
practically on the way, there would be justifiable cause
to pass by the Monastery of Jebel Qarantal.

From far down in the Jordan Valley we could see the monastery, a train of low white buildings preposterously set into the face of sheer rock more than halfway up the Mount of Temptation. Clusters of candle-shaped cypresses shaded us much of the way, recalling the prosperity of the Jericho plain in the first years of the Christian era. Rockstrewn now, and agriculturally impoverished, only these few great trees hinted at the rich balsam groves of ages past, and crossing the torpid, semiarid flatlands between the crumbled walls of Jericho and the rising rock of the mountain, we found little vestige of the lush oasis proudly presented by Antony to Cleopatra, who in turn sold it to Herod the Great.

The circuitous route led us along narrow scarped terraces and dangerously restricted cliffs, past the caverns and caves that had once sheltered the wild animals among which Jesus had lived for forty days. And when at last we reached the monastery, we could readily understand why Satan chose this place to tempt Our Lord with the things of the world, for in those times, with Jericho newly rebuilt and splendid in the plains below and all the lands to the horizon a luxurious panorama of wealth and prosperity, this vista must have been Satan's cleverest snare.

"What secrets *this* mountain could tell us," one of the students commented, and his remark set every imagination among us to work: Jesus and Satan together on the summit. Could there ever have been a more incongruous meeting!

Not by bread alone does man live—so Jesus answered the Tempter—*but by every word that proceedeth from the mouth of God.*

One could not help thinking the mildly blasphemous thought: Suppose, just suppose, Christ *had* accepted Satan's offer at that incredible conference! Today, he would rule only this barren desolation, these stony foothills. There could be no more overwhelming irony or better proof that indeed man does not live by bread alone.

Quietly, one of the boys began an ancient Syriac hymn

of praise and adoration, and one by one as if on cue, we each took up the singing until our paean echoed resoundingly through the hundred hollow caves and recesses that had sheltered so many unnamed monks, ascetics, martyrs, down through the centuries.

As any sensible fellow might have predicted, by the time we reached the plain again we were exhausted. Then digging from our pockets money that was only pennies below the established price, we were able to engage a carriage for our return to Jerusalem.

The carriage was little more than a huge and cumbersome wooden cart affixed with thick splintery boards along the sides, and bucking and bouncing along the none-too-smooth road of the Wadi el-Qelt, we wondered if the temporary ease of our feet was worth the joggling torture to back and buttocks.

The driver had not stopped talking since the trip had begun. He bragged of his mules and complained of the cost of feeding them. He boasted of the money his son made constructing the potash plant and derided the company for trying to get anything out of such a salty sea. After a while, the students paid him no attention whatsoever, intent instead on preparing their explanation for the Bishop as regarded their errant travels.

But at one spot along the jolting, twisting road, the driver insisted upon their attention and pointing to the rubble-strewn remnants of a structure once situated in this isolation, announced that they had arrived at Khan-al-Ahmar, where the good Samaritan brought the robber's victim for rest and treatment. The standing masonry and mosaics were medieval, the remains actually of a crusader's memorial church, but below were to be seen ancient cisterns, hewn into the rock, which had supplied water to man and beast since Biblical times. And even though each youth among them had been raised within the rough perimeter of the Holy Land, there are still those sites and scenes such as this one which rippled the scalp with awe at the thought of the physical closeness of the Gospel's reality.

The carriage moved on. The road twisted again and was now menaced on either side by rising rock. A Bedouin climbed with his small flock of goats among the clefts and crevices where the animals sought scant pastures of rank grass.

"Never at night would I travel this road alone," the driver told us. And wide-eyed youths looked about and saw why: even in daylight there were plenteous nooks and coverts where a highwayman might hide.

"Nothing but evil could exist in a place like this," remarked one of the students.

"You are pessimistic, my friend," said another, "for surely there is good reason for everything."

"Not for such haunts as these," the first insisted. "What reasons could such eerie caves have that was good?"

"Well . . ."

"You see!" the first said with a laugh. "You cannot offer *one!*"

Another intervened. "To hide things in. There's one."

"Hide things?" the first echoed. "Hide things like what?"

And now another joined in: "Remember Timothy?"

"Saint Timothy? You mean to say he hid things out in caves?"

"No. Timothy I, the Catholicos. Yeshue, that's your specialty. Tell this smart fellow the story."

Embarrassed, I searched my mind and shyly at last asked, "What story?"

"About Timothy and the books in the cave. You recall how it impressed you at the time? You said you yourself had seen monks sealing manuscripts up in the side of a mountain."

And the story came back to me from the writings of an eighth-century prelate who had heard of an Arab whose hunting dog had accidentally discovered ancient writings in a cave. The prelate had then conducted a search for these writings, hoping to find the words: "And he shall be called a *Nazarene*" in one of the Prophets.

His search, however, was in vain.

"It is probably just a legend," the first student countered. "And, anyway—what's this business about you watching monks burying books or what have you?"

I told him the story from my childhood, from my days at the Monastery of St. Malky in the Tour-Abdeen mountains. But the other boys, who did not remember the hunger, the disease, the whine of Kurdish rifles, or the scent of death, found humor in my tale, and someone even suggested that I was gifted with a wild imagination.

And it may be so—for as the carriage lumbered through the rocky wilderness, I envisioned in every cave we passed the writings that Timothy had sought a thousand years before, because as I had spoken a moment earlier, I recalled another aspect of the story: they had been seen in a cave *not far from Jericho!*

Arriving in Jerusalem, we reported sheepishly to our Bishop. He kept us waiting for a tensely nervous hour. When at last we were given audience and had begged his forgiveness for overstaying our appointed limits, one of the more eloquent among us explained how we had wished to tread "the very ground where John had preached his rugged gospel of repentance." If the Bishop was indulging us, he masked his humor with a sternly formidable visage and dismissed us only after stirring in our breasts something of that spirit of self-criticism which must have come over John's audiences of old.

Father Salahy was less easily persuaded of our noble intentions. "Taking such things upon yourselves may warrant a more *rugged* gospel right around *here*," he said curtly. "And even visiting those other priories should not have taken two and a half days."

"But, Father," one student protested. "There was also the delay with Michael—"

Michael's eyes turned to the speaker. "I—I wanted to see the Dead Sea closer, Father," he said quickly. "I am responsible for some of the delay."

The bell rang, calling us to evening prayers.

"Well, you *are* all back," the good priest told us, "And it is time for compline. I will keep the matter in consideration, though discipline and obedience are the cornerstones of both proper students and proper monks. Now, off to chapel!"

In the corridor, Michael spun around to face the fellow who had nearly reported his collapse. "It was only the heat," he said insistently. "It could have happened to anyone."

"But you looked very sick," the other replied. "I didn't mean to blame you—"

"I am preparing for the priesthood," Michael said flatly, "and I do not wish to miss my classes while bothersome doctors fuss over me." Then he turned and walked quickly away.

"No one thought to mention our ideas about a monastery in honor of Saint John," someone observed; and the boy who had accompanied me to Kalia sensibly suggested that Father Salahy would probably be in a more receptive mood tomorrow.

In the chapel, I thought of the old monks at St. John's and prayed that such a monastery might truly be raised up, but my prayers were annoyingly disrupted by a young man across the aisle where the very new boys sat. He kept glancing back, a strange half smile showing beneath a dark and winking eye. Thinking he was trying to contact someone behind me, I turned and found only serious students properly at their prayers. Again he turned and winked and smiled—this time full face. My jaw fell open in astonishment, for the other dark eye shot off in a different direction. It was Butros Sowmy, my erstwhile friend from Adana; Butros, the friendly agitator—right here in St. Mark's Monastery!

After compline, I was able to spend a few moments with him in the corridor before the bell called us to our separate dormitories and to bed.

"Yes," he told me. "My brother and I and Boulos Gelph are here. We learned all there was to learn at the orphanage, so Father Dolabani arranged our transfer. Abraham was a little reluctant, but I told him that even a goat cannot graze in the same pasture all its life."

"And"—the possibility stunned me— "are you thinking of taking vows, Butros?"

Butros grinned, the old enigmatic, cocky grin. "Who knows?" he answered. "At least here there is always a roof and the next meal. It is worth thinking about." The bell sounded its call to quarters. Butros leaned closer and winked one wild eye. "There is a window near my bed which drops to the street; I may be able to see both sides of life before I make a decision."

A few moments later, as the moon spilled in upon the sleeping students around me, I could not keep the smile back that crossed my face—it might betimes border upon the scandalous, but with Butros in the monastery, life would hardly be dull!

As it turned out, my thoughts that night were uncharitably presumptuous, for a fierce maturity was not long in catching up with young Butros and in the year that followed he displayed a progressively sharpened mind. True, he was still the source of frequent argument and battle, but they were intellectual or vocal now; for Butros was, and always remained, intensely enamored of that particular form of chauvinism which passes for religious fervor in lands where nationality and religion are regarded as one and the same.

In 1926, the monastery was honored by a visit of His Holiness, Mar Ignatius Elias III, Patriarch of Antioch and all the East. Though all eyes during the incoming procession should have been upon this wise and saintly man whose consecration as patriarch stretched back in unbroken succession to the founding of the Holy See of Antioch in A.D. 37, still for Butros and his brother, and for Boulos and myself there was a special and happy cynosure amid the regal proceedings. Yes, for there among the Patriarch's impressive retinue was our own beloved Father Dolabani.

"So you are Father Hanna's orphans," the Patriarch said after the priest had arranged a private audience and, stricken with shyness before him, we could only nod.

"Well, you seem pretty big for orphans," he said warmly, and Father Dolabani's quiet smile set us immediately at our ease.

"I am told you all have impressive records as students here in St. Mark's. May I look forward to your consecration in the spring?"

There was the question—put directly. Were we willing to relinquish the world and its pleasures? Did we love and honor God and our church enough to put their holy needs before our own? Could we be sure of our fidelity to the ancient restrictive vows of poverty, chastity, obedience? Had we been genuinely called? Had we been chosen?

All the talk and conjecture of the dormitory and schoolroom fell away now like so much idle gossip. The Patriarch's calm eyes searched out our own, and we knew that the question had finally been asked and an answer had to be given. The three of us looked from one to the other to see who would speak first, but the good Patriarch guessed our predicament. "Do not reply now, my sons," he said kindly. "Go alone to quiet places. Think and pray. Our Blessed Lord will let you know your separate answers."

We knelt for his blessing, and as his hand rested paternally upon each forehead, he observed that the hood and habit of the monk would change us not at all—only a mortification of the passions and a tested moral fortitude could turn us into religious worthy of the name. "He who seeks anything else in the monastic life besides God," he concluded, "will find only unhappiness and discontent."

After much soul-searching prayer, Abraham decided he had not been called. Butros, Boulos Gelph, and myself, however, with trembling humility, were among those professed at the next ordination.

All night long we young men had prayed and fasted; but kneeling in the chapel now, our faces illuminated with happiness and hope, no trace of physical exhaustion could be sensed. From a small but ornately framed ikon, the crucified Christ looked out upon the tiny church glittering with the dancing reflections of innumerable candles and heavy with clouds of spicy incense. There were readings from the inspiring poetry of the psalms and then in brilliant scarlet vestments, Mar Ignatius began once more the timeless, endless sacrifice of God for man.

Still in the cassock and white surplice of our noviate, we knelt at the altar. In front of each of us was the folded robe and hood, the habit that would make of us, externally at least, a monk professed of Christ and his holy church. Behind us the stirring hymns raised the hackles of our scalps. There was a sacred and delicious terror in taking so irrevocable a step.

Then the Patriarch blessed the habits and placed upon our heads the black, flat silken caps of the Order of Saint Anthony of Egypt. Twelve white crosses, one for each apostle, graced the crown of the cap and a long silken band hung forward, across the shoulders. Soon, with prayers and rituals steeped in the centuries, this band would be flung back, just as through this ceremony, each man would fling all worldly things behind him.

And should He choose to speak now from his cross within the ikon, what would he say to these young men assembled here? No need to guess, for he had spoken already, and his Evangelist, Saint Luke, had put it down to echo over every generation:

If anyone wishes to come after me, let him deny himself and take up his cross daily, and follow me. For he who would save his life will lose it but he who loses his life for my sake will save it.

I felt the band brushed back behind my shoulders but the colors, the celebrants, the candles, blurred before my eyes. I could not restrain my tears; they sprang forth from unspeakable joy.

"And now," Father Salahy said good-naturedly, "it is time you went to work for a living."

Perhaps the good priest thought it work, but for me the assignment as Monastery Librarian proved to be day upon day a source of enthusiastic happiness. The library at St. Mark's was the depository of fascinating documents: ancient edicts and decrees from the early centuries of the Ottoman Empire, hundreds of invaluable Syriac manuscripts and scrolls made from the hide of gazelles, inscribed in the graceful estrangelo script, an ancient Aramaic form reserved for Scripture. Here too were manuscripts that could only be described as works of art, so superb their illuminated illustrations. Yes, Father Salahy was always gracious enough to think I was *working* in the library; it would have been impolite to disillusion him by revealing that every hour spent there was for me awesome adventure.

"Have you deserted my class altogether, Brother?"

I looked up startled. Only this charming, brusque American would so easily break the silence of the library.

"I'm sorry, Father Charles, is it time already?"

"Time and then some," he replied with a grin. "Our class is over. I'm on my way to your Patriarch's diwan."

I apologized and by way of explanation offered the priest a view of the manuscript in which I had been immersed. Around the larger introductory letters, delicate cherubs cavorted among blossoms as brightly fresh as if they had only now bloomed upon the pages.

"It *is* beautiful, Brother," the priest observed.

Almost jealously, I rewrapped it. "I can never look at these illuminations," I said, "without marveling that those ancient scribes could possess such imaginations — the poetry, the fantasy, they were able to envision, despite the humdrum world in which they lived!"

"Full many a flower is born to blush unseen."

"What?"

"An English poet. You would have heard more of him today had you been in class."

"I am sorry, Father," I replied. "It won't happen again."

"I hope not, Brother Samuel. You are practically the

liaison man for St. Mark's, and I expect you'll need all the English I can give you and then some."

"It is good of our Episcopal brothers to share you with us, Father."

"Thanks, but I'll take your appreciation out in classroom hours."

"I'll be there tomorrow, Father. And on time."

The priest started out. "Oh, by the way, Brother, that manuscript you unearthed—on eleventh-century life in Jerusalem—"

"Yes?"

"Well, I know you're busy enough with the library here and running the Hikmat magazine, but I've been thinking about it ever since you showed it to me. Perhaps we could work together on its translation and publish it in English. That is, if you have the time."

I grinned with pride at the offer. "I shall find time, Father. I shall make time."

The priest raised a cautioning finger. "Outside of class, eh?"

I laughed. "Yes, Father Charles, outside of class."

The Clerical Institute, or Day School, which the Patriarch had established at St. Mark's, became under Father Dolabani's admirable direction a vital organ of the monastery's contribution to the people of Jerusalem. Both cleric and layman were able to avail themselves of many studies, such as English under Father Charles Bridgeman, which had hitherto been proscribed. But St. Mark's revitalized place in the affairs of the community also demanded more and more interrelationships with the official agencies of the government, and though I was able through the Institute to pursue even further my study of the Syriac tongue, my liaison duties took me more frequently from the tranquil solitude of my beloved library and the day finally came when I had to leave it altogether.

The scrawny novice had run in, called my name, and just as hastily, exited. By the time I reached the front desk, there was only a slip of paper to prove he had been there at all. I picked it up and read it. It was a summons to appear in the Patriarch's office at a specific time that afternoon.

I ran my fingers along the paper's edge searching my mind for anything I had done that might warrant a reprimand. I could not recall anything particular but there was still enough of the schoolboy lingering at the edge of my manhood to feel uneasy at such a sudden call to high official circles. A few moments later, however, when the most animated Michael I had ever seen came bounding into the library smiling irrepressibly, my fears were put to rest.

"We are going to Egypt, Yeshue. Egypt, can you imagine?" Then he realized that I had not yet been informed and was dismayed that perhaps he had spoiled the Patriarch's surprise. I assured him that the Patriarch would always think *he* was the first to tell me, and then Michael explained that he and I had been picked for special studies in philosophy, theology, and history. We were going to the Coptic Seminary in Mahmasha, Cairo, for the next two years! My delight and astonishment remained as fresh two hours later when the Patriarch officially informed me.

When Butros heard of this, he lost no time in arranging an audience with the Patriarch, and from his smiling return we could tell that he had been successful. Gently pushing him to the edge of flattery, Michael and I asked him why he had been so anxious to go, of all places, to Egypt.

One eye sought Michael's out, one stayed on me. "Why not?" he quipped with a crooked grin. "I've never been to Egypt."

And so, in another ancient arena of the original apostolic church, we pursued our studies further, considering philosophically and theologically the source of our rites and revelations, learning to love the brotherly bonds that have, since antiquity, made us one with the Coptic, Ethiopian, and Armenian Churches and pondering the pale, almost imaginary differences of phrasing and terminology that have separated us technically from the imposing body of

Western Christianity whose Patriarch quite rightfully sits in Rome. How often in our evening conversations we would voice the wish that would undo the knots of contention, more political than religious, which have crimped the free flow of worldwide Christianity since A.D. 451. That year, objecting more to its improprieties of action than to any declaration of faith, the Syrian Church of Antioch felt obliged to reject the validity of the Council of Chalcedon. How often, hopeful of the ultimate unity of Christians everywhere, we longed for that astute, inspired mind who would dispense with the semantic difference of *person* and *nature* and brush away the mere logomachy that our dividers thrive upon. And our long, long thoughts and spirited conversations would lead us at last to welcome beds but not without a prayer that one day we might see the old strifes healed and the mystical body, now rent, distracted and torn, united once again in all its parts.

In those days also we seized every opportunity to visit the antiquities of Egypt both in museums and at their original sites. We explored Pharaonic tombs and examined the parchment collections in the great city's many libraries, stood in awe within the Jewish synagogue raised near the spot where Jesus and Mary took shelter in their flight to Egypt, and with worn-out, weathered little cameras photographed from every angle the famous Hanging Church, the Mu'Allaka, the oldest, most important Coptic Church in Cairo.

Bishop Isidorus El-Saddi was our constant adviser and informant. Of Syrian origin like ourselves and once a resident in St. Mark's, he treated us with every paternal consideration, and since he himself had founded *Zion*, an important publication of no small merit, my own magazine experience in Jerusalem gave us even more in common. He never tired of answering my queries about some ancient site or manuscript I had seen, or if he could not do so himself he would readily find some other learned friend to lighten the gloom of my ignorance. And between the challenging scholarship offered in the seminary classes and the fascination of the antiquities that surrounded us on every side, my years in Egypt made upon me an unforgettable impression, but it was a rather accidental development there that was to haunt me for much of my life ahead.

Tired after long hours of study in the seminary library, I walked slowly down the cool, quiet hallway toward my room. Passing the cell next to my own, I heard my name called softly. I stopped and looked inside.

"Did you call, Michael?"

"Yes. Back already? I thought you were going to be up all night."

"No, thank God. I finished earlier than I thought."

"You'd better start getting more rest, Yeshue, or they'll think back in Jerusalem that our Coptic brothers didn't feed us. There's no reason for everybody to be as thin as I am."

"Oh, I'm fine, Michael. I get enough rest."

"Well, I hope so. Oh, on the table by your bed—I put a magazine there. I remembered your story coming back from Jericho and I thought you might find this interesting. Let me know what you think about it. Ah—in the morning, if you please. Good night, Yeshue."

"Good night, Michael."

I entered the small room and lighted the lamp. Above the simple, narrow cot, the Crucified seemed to nod in welcome. I set my burden of books upon the table and picking up the magazine, settled into the wooden chair.

It was a scholarly magazine, heavy reading at the end of a long, busy day. Perhaps it could wait until tomorrow. I flicked through it, wondering which article had caught Michael's eye. There seemed to be little here of any pertinency, just the usual dry subjects over which scholars interminably ... but wait, some phrase there, a word or two—I found the page. Yes, yes! No wonder! *Good* for Michael!

It was an article on the teacher Origen, born in Alexandria in A.D. 185 and martyred for his beliefs sixty-nine years later in the prison at Tyre. The article dealt primarily with his tremendous undertaking, the Hexapla, which was a compilation of Old Testament texts as they appeared in Hebrew and five varying Greek translations, but lost in one of the ponderous paragraphs on the sources of Origen's versions was a single sentence that sent a shivering along my spine. Speaking of one such version, the author remarked: *Origen found it in an earthen jar near Jericho in the reign of Antonius Severus.*

I pressed my palms against my temples as if I would force to the surface of my mind all germs of prior knowledge on Origen and the Hexapla. Then I bounded from the chair, out into the corridor and down through the silent, shadowed halls.

The sleepy monk in charge of the library was not at all happy to see me, but shaking his heavy keys ostentatiously, he gave in to my supplications and allowed me a few more minutes among the books.

History . . . Church . . . Eusebius. One . . . three . . . four . . .

The sixth volume. I thanked the weary old librarian, and clutching the book to my breast, I sped again to my cell.

And there it was:

"In this thorough fashion, Origen searched out sacred books. He learned Hebrew and acquired the Old Testament books in Hebrew in the possession of the Jews. He went very deeply into the whole matter of Greek versions of Scripture made by translators other than the Seventy and amongst these he discovered versions by Aquila, Symmachus, and Theodosius which had long remained in obscurity, their translators being equally obscure individuals. He mentioned that one particular version he found at Nicopolis, and the rest at another spot.

"In his versions of the Psalms, now a fifth appeared along with the well-known ones. He went on to point out that there was actually a fifth, a sixth, and a seventh before him. He informs us that one of these was found . . . was found . . .

"Near Jericho . . . in a jar . . . in the reign of Antonius Severus. All these he collected together and made a—"

But I could read no more. The implications were dizzy-

ing. Origen had found his psalms in a jar sometime in the
third century, and the Catholicos Timothy was looking
for works of the prophets five centuries later in a cave —
and both men spoke of Jericho! What if these works still
existed? Books that could speak across the centuries from
the days of Christ himself?

Trembling with some curious agitation, I darkened the
lamp, then knelt and prayed and at last was in my bed.
But my eyes stayed wide, scanning the edges of the moon's
square pattern on my wall, and I knew I would not sleep.

Happy news awaited us on our return to Jerusalem. The
church authorities had given serious consideration to our
suggestions for a monastery to honor Saint John the Baptist.
Some funds had been made available by the church and
the rest was being sought from laity subscriptions. With
spirited enthusiasm we threw ourselves wholeheartedly
into the campaign, though for myself it meant once more
postponing the deeper studies in archaeology that had
become my private dream. Still, even among the busy days
of that period, I could not hear of an ancient book or manuscript without trying to get my hands on it, and if, as often
happened, I could not read such works, there was for me
nonetheless a deep delight in examining them and con-
jecturing upon their sources or the circumstances that
surrounded their origin.

I paced back and forth in the anteroom of the Bishop's
offices. I was fuller of face and figure now, and my beard,
traditional among the monks and priests of the Syrian confession, was black and full, giving me an air and appearance
of maturity that seemed impressive. Only I knew that a
dreaming boy bubbled behind the mask.

Nervously, I rubbed my hands together and prayed that
the Bishop would not think me presumptuous for the request. There were a dozen good reasons to deny it I knew:
the fund-raising campaign for the new monastery demanded experienced liaison men with the official agencies, and the new printing press, well provided with ex-

cellent type for working in Syriac, Arabic, and the European languages, required competent editors and linguists. Again, there was the ever-present shortage of monks, a sorrowful dearth of vocations that was reflected in the rolls of every Christian church as the twentieth-century world wooed more avidly the material and the transitory. Perhaps I was wrong to ask. Perhaps I was wasting the Bishop's time, and my own as well. Why should the good man even consider releasing me for years of study in the archaeological field? If I had wanted to be a scientist, I should have pursued it from the start. Poverty, chastity, obedience, do not reckon with personal ambition. Perhaps I myself should think on it more deeply before presenting my petition. For a moment, I studied the open door leading to the corridor. If I simply left, returned to my duties—but my desire burned and would not be allayed.

"The Bishop will see you now, Brother."

And it was too late to leave. The door of the office was ajar, and Bishop Mar Cyrilos Anton sat smiling graciously behind a huge polished desk cluttered with the paperwork attendant upon his many duties.

"Your Eminence—"

"Good morning, Brother Yeshue, good morning. You've put on a few pounds, I see."

I blushed, my nervous fingers tugging at the cincture around my waist. "The Syrian cooking here, Your Eminence. It must agree with me more than that of our Coptic brothers."

The Bishop smiled again, shuffled some papers and picked up a yellow sheet. "Do you enjoy curry, Brother?"

"Curry, Bishop?"

"Yes, Indian curry. Rice, chicken, spice, et cetera."

"Why, I—"

"It doesn't matter, my boy. You'll learn to like it in any case." He proffered the yellow paper. It was a telegram. "Yes, from the Patriarch himself. You must have made quite an impression upon His Holiness."

Dumbfounded with surprise, I scanned the wire. The

Patriarch Elias III was undertaking a tour of the churches
in India and requested for assignment as his Syriac-lan-
guage secretary, Brother Yeshue Samuel. He was to join
the Patriarch immediately in Mosul.

"Well, my son, and what do you think of that?"

I returned the telegram. "I'm—I'm very honored, Your
Eminence."

The Bishop rose and came around beside me. "So are
we all at St. Mark's. And we shall miss you."

I dropped to my knees, feeling the fatherly hand upon
my head in benediction. I kissed the Bishop's hand in a
gesture at once symbolic of honor, affection, and obedience
to authority. Then I rose and started out.

"Oh, Yeshue," the Bishop called. "And what was it
you wanted to see *me* about?"

I turned back, then quickly glanced away. "Nothing important, Your Eminence. Nothing that—cannot wait."

On February 13, 1931, I departed for Mosul, which was
now in the newly created state of Iraq, and it was a curious
sensation to be speeding back through countryside very
much like that which I had known in Hilwah so many years
ago.

As the minarets and domes that crown the vast walls of
that aged city rose up against the hazy morning skies, and
to the east the mountain ranges climbed higher and higher
up from Jebel Maqlub to the Hakkari ranges of the Persian
border, a glow of distant beauty hovered above Mosul,
evoking the traditions of wealth and magnificence with
which it once rivaled Baghdad. But like much that is
touched with glamour, it could not stand too close an in-
specting eye, for coming nearer one saw that the walls
were crumbling, the gates half ruined, and that despite an
industrial prosperity, squalor reigned.

The people of Mosul seemed busy and colorful nonetheless, with white-turbaned Molla, black-turbaned rabbis,
dark-robed priests, and myriad crowds of noisy soldiers,
careless swinging Arabs, and lounging merchants. The

Patriarch's quarters were at St. Thomas Cathedral. Though offering little consolation to the spirit during Mosul's damp, dismal winter, it advantageously separated His Holiness from the clamor and filth of the city's streets.

Weeks of hectic preparations followed, and day after day the Patriarch's diwan (or headquarters) was crowded with consuls and bishops stung with urgency, as well as local petitioners who sought their leader's aid before his journey took him from their midst. And as each day ended, the strain seemed more visible upon the face of the aging Patriarch.

The last audience over and done with, the Patriarch sighed audibly and removed his miter. It rested upon the chaise longue like a huge black-satin onion. He rose and crossed to the window, and except for his red cassock, the beautiful cross, and the jeweled ikons hanging on thick gold chains upon his breast, he might be in his simple black cloak or *abba,* just a simple priest of God.

"Night falls quickly in the East," he remarked quietly.

From my desk in the corner, I looked up. "It does, Your Holiness."

The Patriarch sighed again and came back into the room. "Ah, well," he said with a smile, "at least it will be warm in India."

"It will, Your Holiness."

The Patriarch raised a hand to my shoulder. "We are glad to have you here, Yeshue," he told me. "You have a calmness of spirit that we will draw heavily upon in the days ahead." I knelt for his apostolic blessing.

"Go now, my son," the Holy Father told me with a gesture of dismissal, "to your supper, your prayers, your sleep. Today has been long enough and tomorrow we commence our journey."

"May I accompany you to your apartment, Your Holiness?"

The Patriarch tapped at his beard and went behind the great desk. "No. We will stay awhile. We wish to examine once more the reports from Mar Julius."

"But it is quite late, Your Holiness, and you've not had supper yourself. Also, your doctor was—"

The Patriarch eased into the chair, already selecting the documents he would require. "We know. We know. We did not wish to see him. He will only tell us the same thing, Yeshue, day after day, the same diagnosis."

"He said it was imperative that you rest as much as possible."

"Did he indeed? And did he also say we should not make the trip?"

"He has given up in that regard, Your Holiness."

A weary smile furrowed the old man's cheeks, pleated the corners of his clear dark eyes. "It would do him no good to persist in that; we have told him so. Here is a chance for us to breach a gap of more than thirty years—a gap that ever threatens schism if not heresy. It would be treason to Our God and to ourself to pass it by. No, Yeshue, let the good doctor treat the bruises of the sheikhs and agas as he sees fit. Our business is healing the wounds of the Holy Church, and we dare not lose a day."

I departed, closing the great door easily so as not to disturb the tired shepherd who had intently set himself to the work at hand, encircled in the lamp's soft coral glow. And much, much later in the night when I—my sleep disturbed by some aberrant and forgotten dream—looked out upon the courtyard, dark and silent now, I saw the lights of the zealous laborer still burning in the Patriarch's diwan.

The following morning, the traveling party, amid much last-minute scramblings for additional luggage and documents overlooked, assembled for the journey. There was another monk besides myself, Father Kiryacos Tannourji, the Patriarch's bodyguard, a secretary, a lawyer, and Archbishop Mar Clemis and, of course, showing no sign of the brevity of his night's sleep, and delightedly alert, Elias III, the one hundred and nineteenth Patriarch of the Holy See of Antioch, spiritual inheritor of a sacred jurisdiction that reached back through the ages to the apostolic times and thence directly to Our Lord and Savior, Jesus Christ. The problems facing the church in India were complicated and would demand all the diplomacy and wisdom the saintly man could muster, but as we started out his cheerfulness and bright spirits were contagious and gave scant evidence of the challenge that lay ahead. But new troubles continued to break out and when negotiations for a reconciliation were at last arranged, the British Viceroy, Lord Irwin, personally appealed to His Holiness Patriarch Elias III to come himself to India and reunite his church. It was in this world of canonical chaos that we found ourselves immersed throughout the spring and summer of 1931.

But a journey of such historic import by so eminent a leader as the Patriarch was not, of course, without its gayer moments. In New Delhi, the British Viceroy lodged and entertained us; in Baghdad, we had an audience with King Faisal; in Cochin, the old rajah received His Holiness from his sickbed, and the Easter services in that district drew crowds so large that the church was unable to accommodate them.

At last we arrived in Travancore, which lies along the lush Malabar coast, rich in spices and coconuts, elephants and ebony, and there we were given a reception by the Maharani which, in the all but embarrassing lavishness characteristic of the schizophrenic economy of India in those days, rivaled the fetes of the Arabian nights. And everywhere, the Patriarch was welcomed with esteem and affection by enthusiastic crowds. Often, the old man had to turn away from his people lest they see the tears of joy and love that brimmed over upon his cheeks.

There was little time for pursuing my archaeology, but in the autumn while visiting the big church in Kottayam known as the Cathedral of the Virgin, it was my especial pleasure to study the pair of ancient stone crosses there which were heavily inscribed in Pahlavi, a form of Persian centuries old. There was a genuine thrill also in discovering that one of these crosses had inscriptions in Syriac as well.

During the year, Patriarch Elias III had spared no effort to mend the rift that divided his congregation. At the Al-

ways Seminary, a touching and momentous reconciliation
between Mar Dionysius and His Holiness had taken place;
and, as far back as early spring, the Patriarch had set in
motion the machinery, which (despite the delicacy of the
situation) came very close to realizing a peace settlement
between the two parties. Through all this he had never
complained. Though the doctor in Mosul had ordered him
to abandon the trip, and though the enervating heat, the
crowds, the wearying rounds of official receptions and ceremonies, had each in turn added to the demands upon his
health and energy, his only thought had been to reconcile
his divided children that there might be, in the evangelist's
perfect phrase, but one flock and one shepherd.

As it turned however, Patriarch Elias III was not destined
to see the realization of this cherished dream. On Saturday,
February 13, 1932, God decreed that the Patriarch's pilgrimage on earth should close at last. We did not know it
then, of course, but another thirty years would pass before
the Syrian Church in India was again restored to unified
order.

Throngs of heartbroken men and women, Christian and
non-Christian, paid homage at his funeral. He was buried
near St. Stephen's Church in Manjinakara, near Kochan-
cherry, and a chapel was raised to mark the spot. To this
day the anniversary of that holy man's death is marked by
the pilgrimage of thousands, many of whom walk more than
two hundred miles to attend the memorial services held in
his shrine.

Sheer busyness and attention to detail did much to
assuage our deep sorrow at the Patriarch's loss to us. All
bishops had to be contacted and a synod arranged to elect
his successor to the See of Antioch; in *locum tenens,* the
Archbishop of Homs became head of the church.

I stayed on at St. Stephen's in Omalloor, stricken with
grief, trying desperately to resign myself to the will of a
Providence which had seen fit to deprive me of paternal
love at the age of seven and which now again, in my young
manhood, in a foreign land, had reached out once more

and left me bereft of the man who had long been my spiritual father. The Apostolic Delegate Metropolitan Mar Julius Elias was my chief source of strength and consolation during those days of my soul's testing, and years later I would encounter the words of an English poet that may have echoed the meaning Christ intended me to read into that trying time: "All which I took from thee," the poet has the Lord of Heaven say, "I did but take, not for thy harms, but just that thou might'st seek it in My arms."

The Metropolitan and I walked a good distance out from the city. Here on the summit of a low rising field it was possible to look back and see the narrow steeple of St. Stephen's needling the evening sky. Long, fleecy clouds clustered along the horizon; tomorrow again promised to be a sweltering day.

"I suppose I will be returning soon, Your Eminence."

The Metropolitan stopped and leaned upon his walking stick. "My brother, of course we will. I was lost in my thoughts and had no idea we'd come so far."

"No, Your Eminence. I meant: I suppose I will be returning to Jerusalem. To St. Mark's."

"That will depend on you, my son."

"In what way, sir?"

"Did His Holiness say nothing to you before he died?"

"There wasn't time. His hand shot to his breast. He cried, "My heart!" and toppled. By the time the doctor—"

"I know, I know. I mean prior to that tragic hour. Did he not tell you of the plans he had concerning you?"

"We had—we had spoken of the priesthood, Your Eminence."

"It was his fondest hope for you, my son. And now—"

"I am not sure, sir. I have thought that perhaps I am best suited for the monastery. Perhaps I should continue in the life to which I first was called."

"Are you afraid, Yeshue?"

"Afraid, Your Eminence?"

"Now that you have felt the fuller burdens of the church, seen the holy weight of its burden upon those who must reconcile it with the vanities of the world. Having seen that during this past year, the tranquillity of the monastery must indeed be tempting."

"I suppose that has touched my thoughts, sir."

"Then think also of this: the church today has great need for her holy monks, but greater still is her need for priests. For learned men, studious men, men who can go abroad among her people and revitalize their faith in her ancient truths.

"It is not an easy life. That is why there is a cross on both the front and the back of the chasuble, that the priest may never forget the passion of Our Dear Lord. It is before him that he may follow in the footsteps of the Christ; it is behind him that he may readily suffer for His sake. Before him, for he must weep for his own sins; behind him, that he will have compassion for the sins of others."

"The monk is near to God, and serves him well, but the priest is in the midst, between God and mankind, serving them both. Yeshue, it was the Patriarch's hope that he might one day ordain you himself. Your studies have already encompassed all but a few months of formal training, and if it is God's will, I would like to fulfill the Patriarch's hope. I would like to ordain you as a priest of God."

On the fourth of April at that same altar on which had been offered the Patriarch's requiem, I knelt before the Bishop's chair and heard his voice softly intoning the wisdom of the holy fathers, the truths of our time-honored doctrines, instructions on how to serve the holy church. Then he arose and took me by the hand. *The Holy Spirit,* so goes the ancient liturgy, *calls you to be ordained a priest.*

We passed through the curtain between the altar and the sanctuary—a token of that veil hanging between ourselves and the heavenly host. The altar steps reflect the ascending ranks of the angels, the altar itself, the tomb of Christ, and the central tablet, or altar stone, speaks of the cross.

Now, like an unborn infant, I was sheltered in the folds of his cape while he prepared in front of him the holy vessels of the Mass.

The chalice veil was parted as the stone was rolled away

from the tomb, but silently fell back in place again, reminding us that the divine mysteries are hidden from the understanding of men, that we cannot comprehend how divinity
and humanity are united in Christ any more than we can
perceive how the bread and wine become the flesh and
blood of God himself. The chalice, the paten, and the spoon
(which recall the tongs used by the angel to place a burning
coal on the lips of Isaiah) were now before him.

Holy is the Father who begets and is not begotten, holy
is the Son who is begotten and is not begetter, and holy is
the Holy Spirit who proceeds from the Father and takes
from the Son—The One True God who redeems us by his
mercy and kindness.

Now, above the vessels and the Holy Elements therein
the Bishop moved his hands, beseeching the assistance
of the Holy Spirit in this grave act of consecration. His
hands grasped at the descending power and wrested it
from the air, and lifting the side of his cape like a great wing
while the music rose in dizzying splendor behind us, he
encompassed my head, my shoulders, my very being, that
this power might be passed to my unworthy self.

When He, the sinless one, of his own Will, prepared to
accept death for us sinners, he took bread in his holy hands,
and gave thanks, and blessed, and sanctified, and broke,
and gave to his holy apostles saying, Take, eat of this for
this is my body which is broken for you and for the many,
and given for the remission of sin and for life everlasting.

And likewise also he took the cup and gave thanks, and
blessed, and sanctified, and gave to his holy apostles, say-
ing, Take, drink ye all of this. This is my blood which is
shed for you and for the many, and given for the remission
of sin and for life everlasting. Amen.

And from the Bishop's fingers I received the Holy Com-
munion, stunned with the overpowering knowledge that
I was, according to the order of Melchizedek, a priest forever.

In the months that I remained there as assistant pastor
at St. Stephen's, I caught frequent glimpses of the crosses

of which Mar Julius had spoken, crosses on *both* sides of the chasuble, but my joy in the priesthood doubled and redoubled nonetheless in my new duties and when, toward year's end, the new Patriarch in *locum tenens* requested my return to St. Mark's in Jerusalem, it was with deep regret that I parted from that saintly man who had shepherded me through the most solemn moment of my earthly existence.

Despite my anxiety to return to my beloved Jerusalem, to my mother and my many long-standing friends as well, I journeyed by way of Mosul that I might have a chance to visit Michael, who had also been ordained since I had last seen him and who was now assigned to the famed Monastery of St. Matthew in the mountains to the northeast of that city.

This was a journey replete with wonders for me, for, as a Syrian, it took me through wide stretches of that country which had once been called Assyria, once inhabited by those warriors of old from whom my people claimed descent. More than seven hundred years before Christ most of the known world had been conquered by her soldiers and her kings. Her capital was Nineveh, "the rejoicing city that dwelt carelessly," a metropolis of unequaled splendor whose downfall had already been predicted. "Woe unto you," cried Nahum. "Woe to the bloody city.... Thy shepherds slumber, O King of Assyria; thy nobles shall dwell in the dust; thy people scattered among the mountains."

Where that great city stood there was now only waste and desolation, and except for a few wretched fields of grain on the banks of the Tigris, the plain seemed entirely barren. Approaching the central levels, however, there was a mound reputed to contain the tomb of the prophet Jonah, around which a little cluster of homes had been constructed. And the glory that was Nineveh is a few scattered fragments of temples and palaces covered by the unlamenting earth; it is a tomb of a prophet who denounced its vices, its only inhabitants a few poor families gathered about his grave site.

But there is one more memory of Nineveh. In the Syrian Church of Antioch about two weeks before Lent there occurs a period of three days solemn fasting during which many of the laity and most of the clergy neither eat nor drink. This is in commemoration of the repentance, all too late, which took place during the seventy-two hours Jonah had announced to be the city's last. In the sixth century, A.D., this fast was instituted as a means of invoking God to end a plague which was ravaging the land, and it is called the Fast of Nineveh as descriptive of both the occasion on which it was established and the severity with which it was to be kept.

Beyond the plain of Nineveh, the mountains loom much closer, and to the north, where the level country lies, I could see scatterings of black tents. A bittersweet longing went out from me. Surely they were the tents of those same nomadic tribes that had herded my father's flocks from Hilwah so many years ago. I was strongly tempted to turn in the direction of those black tents, but the Monastery of St. Matthew was already in sight, clinging like a swallow's nest on the almost perpendicular wall of the mountain, and in the dusty winds sweeping across the plain I seemed to hear the echo of my Bedouin friend's boyhood wisdom. *We journey in the same direction, though we travel by different trails.* I prayed that all was well with him and continued straight ahead.

When, fatigued and breathless, I had at last climbed the steep path scooped out of the rocky precipice, a monk greeted me with the traditional mountain phrase, "Upon my head, you come in peace." And I was escorted to a pleasant diwan at the very top of the building and offered grapes and water while the monk left to prepare the customary cup of coffee.

The monastery, whose physical situation requires that the rooms be built on terraces one above the other, was constructed mostly of the crude concrete and marble that is common in Mosul rather than the hard stone from which the mountain itself is formed, and from the exterior looked roughly made and likely to fall to pieces. It was, however, deftly constructed and, inside, the rooms were clean and comfortable.

I walked to the little windowed balcony and looked out across the monastery grounds. I could see a few trees of fig and apricot and patches of pasture here and there among the rocky slopes on which the monks' small flock were grazing. It was a strange place, almost inaccessible, and though the air was glorious, none but a recluse would have chosen such a spot. Michael, I thought, must be happy here. I felt a renewal of pleasure at the thought of seeing him again.

The monk returned with the steaming coffee and a tray of freshly baked bread. "What brings you so far to Mar-Matthai?" he asked politely. "I have come to pay my respects to Father Michael," I replied.

He studied me for a moment and then dropped his eyes. He made no further conversation until I had finished the coffee. Then with a brief word, he bade me follow him.

We went west of the great gate, past a large cave, from the roof of which a tiny mountain stream dripped continuously. It was thickly shaded in front by fruit trees, and rows of young lettuces peeked from a tiny garden. Nearby, a flourishing row of beehives made of earthenware pots busily hummed with their honeyed activity. Just beyond the huge, plain building that was their church, we turned into a smaller structure which appeared to be a mausoleum; inscriptions indicated that many Syrian bishops were buried there.

The monk paused and said nothing.

"Well," I remarked after a moment, "he doesn't seem to be here, Rahib."

The monk regarded me curiously and nodded in the direction of one of the tombs. "He rests there, good Father," he told me. "We have not yet inscribed the stone."

The air seemed suddenly stale, morbidly offensive. I closed my eyes tightly.

"Did you not know, Father?" the monk asked quietly.

I shook my head.

"He was very young and a holy man. He had not been with us long."

"How did—he die?" I asked.

"We never knew. For three days he was feverish. It seemed to be passing. Then on the fourth morning, we found him—"

I crossed myself and walked out into the sunlight again. "All things are passing," I thought aloud.

"What's that you say, Father?"

"Nothing, Rahib. Just a phrase Father Michael was fond of: *All things are passing. God only is changeless.* Rest in peace, my brother."

There were few monks at Mar-Matthai and, as had been the situation at the Greek Monastery by the Jordan, most of them were very, very old. Still, they were vigorous and proud of their illustrious history. Their monastery had been founded by St. Matthai, a Syrian monk from Abgarshatt near Diarbekir, who had spoken out against the tyranny of Caesar and had sought refuge in these mountains that he might worship his God in solitude. It wasn't long, however, before thousands of ascetics inspired by his example followed him into the crags and crevices. Thus the area came to be called Jebel-Alfaf, the Mount of the Thousands.

Within the main church there was yet another source of the reverence and veneration with which the centuries have steeped St. Matthew's Monastery. In a small shrine known as the House of the Saints is interred one of the greatest of Syrian ascetics and apologists, well-known Mar Gregorious Bar-Hebraeus, a prodigious writer whose works range from a treatise on bells to a universal history of mankind. In the eleventh century, he was our Catholicos of the East.

As in almost all Syrian monasteries, the library offered some excellent copies of his work and some other fascinating manuscripts from the Middle Ages. But the priceless scrolls and treasures that history reveals as having been housed there were lost to Kurdish and Persian raiders hundreds of years before.

"We had many things here once, Father, but we shall not see their like again," the old monk told me. "There was a beautiful manuscript by the monk Mubarak, for example – the entire New Testament by the hand of a gifted artist. I did not see it, but I'm told it was inspiring to look upon."

"Where is it now, Brother?" I inquired.

"We do not know. There was a report that the Syrian Catholic Church in the village of Kara-Kush possessed it. Then we heard that their Metran in Mosul received it from them. I should not be surprised to hear one day that the Vatican now owns it."

At least, I thought, the Kurds will not be raiding the Vatican.

"Centuries ago," he continued, "St. Matthew's also owned the Hexapla. Do you know what that is, Father?"

I smiled as I said yes. How could this simple monk know that Origin's Hexapla and the reports of the Jordan cave had haunted me since my student days in Egypt? He lifted the cover of a huge Syriac manuscript, leafed through the pages, and at last pointed out a beautifully inscribed paragraph.

It was an epistle of Mar Timotheos I, Catholicos of the Eastern Syrian Church (Nestorian), the same man who had sought out the Jordan cave in the eighth century. In this epistle to his Metropolitan Mar Sergius of Elam, he describes how he had had three copies of Origin's work and had returned the original to the Monastery of Mar-Matthai.

The monk closed the book with a sigh. "Now it is only a memory, Father," he said sadly. "All the old things have vanished with the ages."

"So it seems, Brother," I replied, but not without an unspoken prayer that it was not so.

That evening, after a simple but nutritious supper, I returned to my room to read my office, but my prayers had to be forestalled until a later hour, for my mind was abuzz with distracting thoughts and the stark beauty of the mountain view rendered me a prisoner of memory, for the moment unfit for serious proper prayer.

Far over the plains, blue and ruddy now in the steeling twilight, storms were sweeping in quick succession from the east, but westward, over the setting sun, the Sanjaq hills stood out against the sky. From this height I could see the Monastery of Mar Behnam, now in the hands of Syrian monks of the Roman confession who had received us warmly when the Patriarch's party had visited them en route to India.

I could see also the spidery rivers that crookedly cracked the plain, the Guman, the Khazir, the Great Zab, all of which meet at last in the mighty Tigris. Along their banks now, twinkling little lights began to mark the khans and coffeehouses. Some lights moved with the rivers, oil lamps, no doubt, strung up aboard the keleks, the rafts floated upon numerous inflated skins which have borne the trade and traffic in this part of the world since the days of the Assyrians, Cyrus, and Herodotus. And from here, rowdy, boisterous Mosul, despite its many domes and minarets, seemed a small village nestling down for the night.

How apt a spot the monks had chosen for St. Matthew's! Here, of all places, one was far off from the world and its vanities. Here one could hold tryst with one's own soul, perhaps find God himself in the depths of one's own heart.

And when the sun sucked his colors from the sky, the majesty of the mountains subtly increased as the crepuscular haze revealed the many cell-like recesses of the hillside barrens. Easy to see how they had called the stalwarts of old to a life of devotion. Deserted now, they made me think of the Jordan Wilderness and the Mount of Temptation. There, too, the devotees had vanished and the solitary life was practiced only within the shelter of the monastery.

A thin rain began to spit at my window ledge and somewhere a little bell tinkled vespers to the monks and shepherds. I thought again of Michael and of Saint Paul's injunction that we know not the day nor the hour when the

Son of Man will call. I remembered standing with Michael at the pyramid of skulls in Mar Saba. "It is hard to realize," I had remarked, "just how many people have died for the sake of Christ." And he had replied, "Harder to realize, Yeshue, how few people live for him."

Michael *had* lived for Christ, a short but dedicated life, and here in this solemn isolation, he had found a serene and sacred spot in which to await his resurrection.

I could tarry here only a few days, but I relished each hour of contemplation and tranquillity, and ever renewed my gratitude to the late Patriarch whose kindness had originally made my journey possible.

"I am reluctant to leave Mar-Matthai, Rahib," I told the elderly monk who accompanied me to the gate. "These few days have been among the most beautiful in my life."

He nodded his head as though many a departing guest had said the same. "It is because you were close to God, here, Father," he said simply. "Do you agree?"

I did, of course. He smiled and shook my hand.

As I left the gate, he touched my sleeve. "God is not a native of the mountains, Father," he said with a smile. "Take him with you. He is one's natural habitat—wherever one happens to be."

Back in Jerusalem, I was pleased to find that the land for St. John's Monastery had been purchased and that construction was under way. Frequently, business duties would bring me to the site and I could never go out into that rocky, foreboding waste without recalling the stories of Origin and the Catholicos Timothy. Having concluded my errand, I would often stand for a moment looking out across the barren steps and dusty, dry recesses, sensing, I think, some small portion of that spirit of adventure and assurance which Columbus must have experienced as he gazed across the waters to the bright horizon's curve.

In 1939, the Patriarch Mar Ignatius Ephrem I consecrated our own Father Salahy as Mar Philoxenus Jacob,

Metropolitan of Jerusalem, and among his first official functions was the consecration of the chapel in the recently completed monastery. It was a novelty indeed to see the desert roads stirred with the clouds of an automobile cavalcade as parishioners and well-wishers arrived for the ceremonies. We had hoped to see the Greek Orthodox monks from the other St. John's, but true to the old man's prediction, most of them had gone to their eternity since the days of our youthful adventure. It was said that there were now no more than two or three monks in the entire abbey. Our own monastery had been raised just in time, it seemed, to keep the vigil in the wilderness. I found reason to visit there now as often as possible and though I sought out many a dark and humid time-forgotten cave, I never found a clue to encourage my dreams and I wished often for that archaeological acumen that might have aided or at least reasonably channeled my search.

Later that year, however, my interest in old manuscripts was to afford me another opportunity for travel and study. Mar Philoxenus assigned me to serve as companion to an English gentleman and scholar, Mr. Boyd Alexander. He was interested in both the Syriac language *and* the ancient Egyptian monasteries, and he wished to have someone available who would be able to bring to his attention all pertinent Syriac documents in those well-stocked but little-used libraries.

A few weeks later, I found myself in the unique position of feeling our car sink again and again in the sands of the Faran Desert as we approached Mt. Sinai. Even past the sand, the road was little more than a torturous course through the valley beds of dried-up rivers, sided by high walls of stone from which every vestige of flora and fauna had disappeared, except for occasional thorny shrubs. Since the Monastery of St. Catherine, our destination at this point, was more than five thousand feet above sea level, a gradual but consistent upgrade added to the difficulty of travel, and we could rarely move more than a few miles an hour in the baking heat.

Jebel Musa is the traditional location of Mt. Sinai. It is this place which is presumed to be the scene of God's presentation of the Ten Commandments to Moses. There St. Catherine's nestles like a small medieval city on a plateau about midway to its peak. Behind the monastery, the sheer walls of the massif soar to the sky.

About two centuries after Christ, Christians fleeing Roman persecution hid themselves on this plateau, and about eighty years later the first monks to occupy the area sent a plea to Saint Helena, mother of Constantine, begging her protection. She arranged to have a fortress constructed, with a small church inside, and as the fame and veneration of the abbey spread, the increase in both monks and pilgrims necessitated a larger establishment. The foundation of the present structure was laid in A.D. 542 and named in honor of the saint whose relics were found on the Sinai peninsula and subsequently transported to the monastery for safekeeping. Its incredible library houses manuscripts collected here from its earliest days. The largest section is Greek, and Syriac documents follow. Smaller divisions include manuscripts in Arabic, Georgian, Armenian, Coptic, and Ethiopic.

It was in this very library that the German scholar Count Tischendorf made his sensational discovery of the Codex Sinaiticus in 1859. He arranged for the purchase of this fourth-century Greek manuscript through friends in the aristocracy, and following the October Revolution in that country, it was eventually sold to the British Museum for 100,000 pounds. ($500,000). This manuscript, clearly supported by the Codex Vaticanus, showed important differences in the "received text" of the New Testament with all the weight of antiquity behind it. Evident in the Count's story, too, is an example of the incredible luck that sometimes is seen at work in such major discoveries.

While studying manuscripts of a much later period at St. Catherine's, the Count noticed that the monk assigned to the porter work in the library had a number of parchment sheets collected amid the refuse. Inquiring about

them, he was advised that they were on their way to the
small stove that heated the reading room. The Count pulled
them out to study them more closely, and was amazed to
find that they were of a much earlier period than anything
he had seen thus far.

The monk agreed that this might be so, but since they
were in a language unintelligible to anyone there, of what
value could they be? The shocked scholar made the monk
promise that any future "discards" would be shown to
him and agreed upon payment of a silver coin for each one
he found worth keeping. Through the monk's new zeal
in tidying up now, the Codex Sinaiticus was assimilated
and the world of knowledge came to possess the most
ancient complete version of the New Testament.

Since that time, of course, the monks and priests of
St. Catherine's have been much more cognizant of the
precious works in their keeping, and a similar treasure,
another fourth-century Syriac version of the Gospels is
now displayed, carefully enclosed in a beautifully designed
wooden case especially created for it at Cambridge University in England.

Mr. Alexander and I spent our days at St. Catherine's
in studious fascination. From the matin bell until compline,
our hours were steeped in legend, tradition, antiquity.
Early in the morning, hungry Bedouins would assemble
at the base of the north wall of the fortress. There a wind-
lass, centuries old, worked a primitive elevator by which
was lowered freshly baked bread from the monastery ovens.
The nomads by way of repayment would then send up
sheafs of bramble and kindling wood to be used by the
monks for fuel. During the day, taking a respite from our
studies, we would ascend the narrow roadway cut through
the rocks of the mountain to Sinai's chapel-crowned summit. From there, if no mist shrouded the view, we could
discern the Red Sea to the south, and far to the east, the
Gulf of Aqaba. On our way back to the monastery, we
might pause at an ancient monument, a monument to the
brotherhood that must one day, if the world is to continue,

be a universally held concept. Here, midway to the summit, the Greek Orthodox monks have built and maintained a mosque for Muslims that the traveling Bedouins on the Feast of Aaron and other solemn Islamic occasions might also have a place to pray and meditate here on Mt. Sinai's crest.

It was in the library itself, of course, that our most enthralling moments were spent. An elderly monk assigned to our service spared no effort in answering our many questions. On one occasion while pointing out the processes by which the age of a manuscript was determined, after he had explained how the thickness of the vellum, its feel to the fingers, its resistance to being folded, etc., were highly important, he startled us by tearing off a small corner of the page and placing it over the candle that burned before us on the table. Then he bade us to breathe deeply.

"Vellum, leather, parchment, all have a different scent when burned," he explained, "and even these separate scents vary with the ages. It is not an infallible test, but we have come to put much faith on it." He smiled across the table at our surprise. "Of course, if the German scholar had known this, he might have had a stroke when he first stood warming himself by the stove and breathed in the fragrance of the fire."

On our return to Jerusalem, the holocaust that had been threatening the world for a number of years had at last become a reality in Europe. Insofar as Palestine was concerned, the actual war was distant, but with the contracts made available by the establishment of the British Eighth and Ninth Armies, Palestine in general realized a great expansion of its economy. The Jewish community, which was far better prepared industrially, realized huge profits. However, the citrus market (nearly half of which was Jewish) was cut off by the war's activities and suffered so greatly that many years were required for it to recoup its losses.

As always, the presence of major warfare increased in the hearts of men their sense of the brevity of life; and their numbered days made of them more dutiful Christians for a while at least.

Ministering to the faithful and editing the newly established patriarchal magazine absorbed most of my time during the early forties, though now and then some local incident would give us reason to pause and wonder what would become of Palestine once the World War had ended.

Late in 1943, Butros, who had never ceased to keep his ear attuned to the political drums, sat with me over coffee and a late evening cigarette. Before him the newspaper shouted in black headlines the defeats and advances in the European and Pacific theaters.

"The big one will last another year," he told me. "Perhaps two. Then ours will begin."

"Ours?" I echoed.

He flipped the pages of the paper rapidly and stopped at a smaller news item midway through it. "This will affect us more than all the battles the world over that are being fought tonight."

I read the story. A courtmartial board had found two British soldiers guilty of stealing numerous weapons and thousands of rounds of ammunition. They had been accused of selling the loot to the almost mythical Jewish Army known as the Haganah.

"Do you know how much of that they have recovered?" I shook my head.

He held up a finger before his one straight eye. "One bullet, Yeshue. They have recovered one bullet. The Jews are saving the rest to drive us out."

"I can't think that, Butros," I told him. "There is already talk of an organization of nations that will be responsible for things after the war. And of all peoples, the Jews know what the world most needs is religious tolerance and brotherhood."

He despaired of my political acumen. "This will not be religious," he predicted. "It will be geographical. They want Israel, and they will do anything to get it. Mark my words, Yeshue, we will know soon enough where the rest

of that ammunition is. We will hear it singing through the
air."

Butros was my friend and fellow monk, but I credited
much of what he had said to the fierce nationalism that had
always been part of his temperament. Still, late into the
night I lay awake wondering just what would become of
my beloved Palestine, my dear city of Jerusalem. No doubt
the Jews were more than justified in seeking some permanent place as their own. For centuries they have been
scattered across the face of the globe and subjected to unhappiness, persecution, even torture, frequently at the
hands of peoples supposedly Christian. And surely when
they thought of a national homeland, this, their original
home, came to mind with a stunning historic logic. But
what of the Arabs, both Christian and Muslim, who had also
shared in this land for untold generations? It was their
home, their land, as well. What was to become of them?
Were these shores whereon the Prince of Peace himself
had walked to know again the bloody blast of war? I fell
into a fitful sleep, praying it would not be so.

The pressures of office and the world conflicts weighed
heavily upon our beloved Bishop. Illness at last had so
incapacitated him that I was named Patriarchal Delegate
and obliged to shoulder many of the burdens of the diocese.
He did not live to see the peace he longed for with such
fervor.

That peace, itself, did not stay with us long.

The Jews, who had seen their numbers diminished by
millions in the genocidal atrocities of the Third Reich,
were understandably impatient to establish their own
native land; and the Haganah, less and less clandestine as
their demands became more publicly acknowledged, saw
in the vacillating British position the only obstacle to their
success. Britain, however, ignoring world opinion (which
favored the Jews because of what they had suffered under
Nazi brutality), saw in every terrorist attack a reason to
hold on even tighter to her strategic gateway to the Middle
East, over which she had been given the legal mandate

At Jaffa Gate, entrance to Old City of Jerusalem. The author's first entry into Jerusalem as Archbishop, after ordination in Homs, Syria, 1946
Photo copyright by Photo-Ilani

since the end of the First World War.

There were conferences and talks between rival factions in Palestine, but they were not enough. The fruitless conferences while underground forces threatened violence recalled too vividly the talks that had gone on while Poland fell, the talks that had gone on while Czechoslovakia was overrun, the talks that had gone on while they fought with hand and hammer, stick and stone, in the horror of the Warsaw ghetto. Talks had gone on too while the ovens were ignited and the showers of cyanide were released upon mothers, wives, and children. The Jews had had enough of talking. In July of 1946, while conferences were being held in the beautiful King David Hotel, a terrorist bombing took the lives of 91 British, Arab, and Jewish public servants.

The astute might have learned from that the insanity which could lie ahead in Palestine, for this would be a war of curious reversals. The machine gun, the fire bomb, the hand grenade, had not learned selectivity; for in time Jew would as often kill Jew as Arab in an area where enemy and ally had sometimes been neighbors for years. Meanwhile, however, most of the violence was directed against the British, who were generally unsuccessful in seeking out the terrorists.

Shortly before Christmas, 1946, His Holiness consecrated and appointed me Archbishop and Metropolitan of Palestine and Transjordan, and my episcopacy thus encompassed nearly the total arena of the disputed soil. Extremists on both sides made life a tense, uncertain busi-

His Eminence the British High Commissioner's visit to the author at the Monastery of St. Mark, 1946, during congratulatory audience at the time of his appointment as Archbishop of Jerusalem

ness as the winter passed into spring.

It was Maundy Thursday, 1947. The strife that tore apart the Holy Land kept from her shores that year many of the pilgrims who in more peaceful times sought out the especial blessings of the passion here where they were endured and gainsaid. But the age-old ceremonies of the churches go on, as they will forever.

In St. Mark's, as Archbishop, I with my clergy repeated again the act of humility proffered two thousand years ago by Our Lord when he stooped to wash the feet of his twelve apostles, and commemorated the institution of his Last Supper's Sacrament. Likewise, the Armenians, Copts, and Ethiopian priests and monks celebrated these ceremonies in their own churches and, in fraternal goodwill, we made our way down Christian Street en route to the Church of the Holy Sepulcher to pray in our own Chapel of St. Joseph of Arimathea at the site of the Lord's resurrection.

It was a warm afternoon, and though the pilgrim influx was restricted by the temper of the times, refugees more than made up for their absence; the streets of Jerusalem were congested.

The round *kawoog*, the headpiece worn by the archbishop in his official dress, seemed to cut into my forehead, fittingly recalling, as it should, the cloth with which Christ's head was bound for burial. The golden crosier, symbol of my authority, my shepherd's staff as it were, was heavy in my hand. Before me, two strong Kouwases acolytes parted the seething crowds. In other days, these bodyguards were but colorful representations of the dignity of the archbishop's office, but when no one knew from what frenzied hand the next gun might be fired, they were bodyguards indeed, and they marched stoutly as soldiers of the church.

At Hezekiah's Pool, the little procession turned. On Christian Street, approaching the Holy Sepulcher, the crowds seemed to double. From here one could see the attraction — a platform raised in the church courtyard like a medieval stage. There was a throne upon which the

Greek Patriarch would later sit and cushions for the priests who would represent the twelve apostles. Time enough for the people to mourn Christ's death tomorrow; today an almost festive spirit surged over them. The air was redolent with the baking breads and roasting meats with which the street hawkers would assail the attending onlookers.

My guards and I moved closer. My thoughts were suddenly pulled back to another Passion Week nearly twenty years before. Then, as a hungry, ragged child, I had parted the crowds so that my mother might reach this very shrine and fulfill a long-standing vow. And with my mind thus occupied, I did not hear the first call from a man in the throngs pushing beside me — a man with a message that would change my entire life.

BOOK
THREE

Thou hast made the earth to tremble; thou
    hast broken it:
Heal the breaches thereof; for it shaketh.
Thou hast showed thy people hard things:
Thou hast made us to drink the wine of aston-
    ishment.

—From the Sixtieth Psalm

GEORGE SHAYA WAS A MIDDLE-AGED MEMBER OF ST. Mark's congregation. He had been trying to attract my attention for some time and at last through the crowds and beside me, he tugged at his great brush of a moustache and paused for a moment to catch his breath.

"Your Grace, Your Grace," he said. "I have something important to tell you."

"Can't it wait until I return to the monastery?"

"No, Your Grace, because I must get on to Bethlehem if I'm going to do you any good."

I halted the bodyguards. "All right, George," I said with a resigned smile, "what is it?"

He leaned closer. Tobacco thickened his breath. "Bedouins," he told me. "They have some very old writings. Writings in Syriac such as you keep in your monastery. They have brought them to my friend in Bethlehem. He is one of us, and I told him I would speak to Your Grace about them first." "Where did the Bedouins get them, George?" I asked.

"In the desert, in a cave. Near the Dead Sea. They are very, very old, Your Grace. They are wrapped like mummies."

My interest quickened. "When can I see these—mummies?"

"The Bedouins come in only on Saturdays—for the markets. It will have to be then."

The crowds surged around us impatiently. Our little

tête-à-tête was stopping traffic. "All right, George. Bring them to me on Saturday, and we will find out what this is all about." He grinned happily, rendered an awkward bow and salute, and was swallowed up in the surrounding crowds.

A week or more passed before George returned again. This time, he brought with him not Bedouins but another Syrian, a man shorter than himself and darker, with wide wary eyes and a broad fleshy smile. His dress was a curious contradiction of style, for over a long, flowing abba he wore a Western business jacket and his ears protruded comically from under a square red tarboosh pushed tightly down on his head.

George introduced him as Khalil Iskander, or "Kando," a coreligionist from Bethlehem whose business sense had raised him from an itinerant cobbler to a prosperous merchant; his general store, so he said, was the main source of provisions for the Ta'amireh tribesmen.

In the Eastern fashion, we bantered idle conversation over Turkish coffee for what seemed endless minutes; then at last Kando produced from the folds of his robe a newsprint-wrapped package about the size and shape of a bottle of wine. He set it upon the table but did not take his hand from it, and then with great detail and loquacious embellishments, he proceeded to tell me his version of its origin — a story that even divested of his colorful inserts made of myself an awestruck audience.

Some weeks back, he told me, when the tribe was herding its flock of goats down through the rugged ranges near the Dead Sea, one of the animals had become separated from the flock and in the ensuing search, a shepherd boy had come upon an oddly positioned cave into which he feared his kid might have stumbled. He paused in the desert heat to listen for its bleatings, and sensing nothing but the dull, sulphurous silence around him, he picked up a small rock and deftly tossed it into the opening. If his goat was there, he reasoned, such an assault would raise a frightened protest from it.

Entrance to the cave, with the Dead Sea plain in the background. The original entrance is the upper one, left of center. The lower hole is one that was made by the clandestine excavators in the autumn of 1948. The floor of the cave is at the level of the lower hole
Photo courtesy of the American Schools of Oriental Research

When the rock hit, no goat responded. But what the shepherd boy heard was even more alluring. Inside that isolated cavern his rock had struck and broken what sounded to him like pottery!

He edged himself up along the rocks to peer within and all but lost his footing in surprise. Inside were several large cylindrical objects which, as his eyes became acclimated to the gloom, seemed to be jars. Jars such as the women of Palestine used to bring water from the wells — but larger and thicker. A woman could not balance such jars as these, and out here in the wilderness what purpose could they have except to hold treasure? Robber's treasure!

He sped from the cave and rejoined his flock, but the following day he returned with another tribesman and with the courage of company they entered the cave.

Kando pushed the package toward me. "They found no treasure," he said. "Only this."

I contained my anxiety. "Why did they bring it to you, my son?" I asked.

He beamed proudly. "I am their confidant and friend. I am the only one whom they trust. Besides, if nothing else, they thought I might make use of the leather in my cobbling shop."

Leather? I could wait no longer.

It was a bulkily rolled scroll, deteriorated or eaten away at the top and bottom, but even so, nearly ten inches in length. It was brittle and yellowed with age, and there were many cracks in it. Carefully, I unrolled a column about four inches wide. But it was not, as George had told me, in Syriac. The writing before me was undoubtedly Hebrew!

I took a small fragment from a damaged edge and asked for a match. They watched me in mild astonishment as I raised the flame. I could not restrain my smile, thinking how their expressions mirrored my own in the library of St. Catherine's some years before. The fragment darkened, wrinkled, smoldered; a scent of aged burnt flesh lingered briefly in the air about us. It *was* preserved animal skin!

I took another tiny piece and pressed it between thumb and forefinger. It crumbled to dust. It seemed indeed very, very old!

"Can Your Grace read this document?" one of the merchants asked.

"No," I confessed. "It is written in Hebrew."

Kando muttered disappointedly. It was not *his* mistake, he insisted. When the sheikh of the Ta'amireh had brought them to him, he had used an old Arabic expression which said, "Ancient things are in Syriac." He rose to his feet. He had wasted enough of his valuable time. Perhaps George should take them to a Jew somewhere, otherwise—

I interrupted him. "Wait, my friend. I wish to purchase

them. Do not leave just yet."

George grinned in reassured relief. Kando was puzzled. "But if they are not in your language, Your Grace, and you cannot read them, of what good will they be to you?"

"I do not know yet," I admitted. "But I wish to buy them nonetheless."

"All of them?" George asked excitedly.

I hesitated. The others might be anything and from anywhere. In good conscience, I had to realize my friends in this transaction were not above connivance.

"We will see. When can you bring the rest?"

Kando rubbed his hands together and furrowed his brow. It would take time. The Bedouins come to Bethlehem only on Saturdays. He did not know when he would see them next. With a promise of arranging such a showing as soon as possible, the merchants left and it was with a sinking heart that I watched the scroll rewrapped and swallowed back inside Kando's tunic—wondering all the time what it really was, and if I should ever see it again.

Spring vanished and the lethargic summer days fell heavy upon a Jerusalem already heated with the tense factions of the political climate. There was little time to think of Bedouins or merchants' tales of desert discovery. Only at night, after a long day's duties were behind, would my mind return to that curious morning's exchange, and in the shadowed solitude of my cell, I was left to consider the innumerable aspects of what I had seen and heard.

A goat lost in the rocky desert, a shepherd tossing an errant stone, caves and caches—these seemed the fabrics of fiction, did they not? Indeed, perhaps it was all a deceit of some sort and I had not heard from them again because they lacked the courage to go through with it. Perhaps they did not intend to contact me at all. Still . . .

Writings of old had pointed to the existence of stray documents, and was it so improbable that an Arab's dog or a truant goat could accidentally come upon such places every thousand years or so? It was not only probable, but quite natural. Indeed, who else would be out in that wilderness but nomads such as these?

"Somebody," the old monk at St. John's had told me, "somebody was keeping vigil here in the wilderness." And, of course, they would have been Jews! They would have written in Hebrew!

When such thoughts assailed me, sleep did not come easily. When I considered what I might have held that morning, my thumb and finger would itch as though the dust of the crumbled fragment still lodged between them.

On the first Saturday of Tammuz, which in the Julian Calendar that year was July 21, a firm appointment was made for the Bedouins to see me at St. Mark's. Since I was not certain about anything concerning the documents they were to bring and since I did not want to raise the hopes of others at St. Mark's until I was convinced of their authenticity, I mentioned the meeting to no one, but I waited all morning in a slight fever anticipating at every moment the knock on the door of my third-floor apartment.

At noon the markets would close because of the heat. If they had not arrived by then, I must consider the appointment canceled. The morning passed. No one had come.

Anxiety had sharpened my appetite, but I was irritated and discouraged when I entered the refectory for the noon meal. As we dined, I listened with only half an ear to the casual conversation of my fellow priests until at one point Father Gelph mentioned an incident of the morning which caused my spoon to drop clattering to the saucer.

"You did *what*, Father?"

"I sent them away. Oh, first I inspected their so-called manuscripts. They were filthy scrolls, wrapped in sticky linen and stinking of pitch or something. They insisted on seeing you, Your Grace, but I was firm with them."

I bolted from my chair.

"I've been waiting for them all morning," I said curtly.

Father Gelph was confused, and rightly so. After all, he had only done his duty by keeping such "filthy things" out of the monastery, and I had mentioned nothing to him about my appointment.

"Besides, Your Grace, as best as I could make out they were in Hebrew. Probably old Torahs they had found."

I was already at the door. "I understand, Boulos," I told him. "You had no way of knowing." And I sped to my office to telephone Kando's store, leaving behind me a table of gaping priests who must surely have thought that the pressure of office had at last undone their Archbishop.

I did not have to call Kando. He was at the other end of the ringing phone when I entered my office.

The democratic distance of our connection negated my rank as archbishop. Kando had called to scold me, and scold me he did. Why, I had not even offered them a cup of coffee. An Arab could never forgive such disregard for propriety.

I explained to him what had happened, and he in turn said that George Shaya, who had been with the Bedouins, had guessed as much. A lucky thing, too, he said, that George had been there. Otherwise, there would be no scrolls for me at all, for after they left the monastery, they had offered the documents to a Jewish merchant whom they had met in the marketplace beyond the Jaffa Gate. He told them he would gladly pay what they were asking and invited them to follow him to his office on the Jaffa Road. Only at the last minute and by turning the political conflicts to his own advantage was George able to convince them that it was a trick and that they would surely be killed in such staunchly Jewish territory. He persuaded them to return to Bethlehem, and Kando assured me that despite the rudeness and confusion of the morning, I would, as his Archbishop, and through the zealous efforts of George and himself, be given another opportunity to purchase them.

A few weeks later, on August 5, Kando, George, and two Bedouins arrived at the monastery. Again I heard the story of the lost goat and the cave—this time from the boy purported to have discovered it. Then from a wrinkled, soiled bag, Kando produced not one, but *five* aged and ugly scrolls that seemed to me at the moment the most beautiful things in the world.

One was quite thick and excellently preserved, with column after column of clearly defined Hebraic lettering hanging gracefully from ruled lines. Another—that which I had tested on the first visit—was side by side with a similarly yellowed scroll. The fourth was quite decomposed, with a regular break running along one complete side, which made it a few inches shorter than the others. The last was a leather cylinder, hard, black, and brittle; it seemed all but welded together.

"Wasn't it said that they were wrapped in linen?" I asked.

"Perhaps they were," Kando replied archly. "But these things do not hold well in moving. You should have bought them the first time if you wanted their covers as well."

Our coffee arrived, and we sat down to the long discussions that would proceed establishing a price. Going only on guesses and the tales of wandering nomads, I could hardly expect the monastery, which was already hard put upon by the needs of our congregation, to extend any money to encourage my whim; and, despite my office, I was a monk in practice, so my own fortune was a modest one, accumulated over months by a wedding gratuity here or the sale of Syriac textbooks there. My anxiousness to own them, however, had communicated itself to these perceptive men, so that each rising offer was met with the traditional clicking of the tongue which indicated that it was not enough.

At last I opened my desk drawer and brought forth a little chest containing all the money I personally possessed. To pass it to them would mean delaying the publication of the series of Syriac language textbooks which I had been preparing; it would also mean forestalling any meager request my mother might make in an emergency. If I was wrong, it was like burning the money in a fireplace. If I was right, I owed it to my community and to scholarship to offer everything I had.

I took out the notes and placed them on the edge of the desk.

"That is all the money I have in the world, my friends," I told them. "I can offer no more than that."

Kando's electric fingers snapped it up, and practiced thumb to lip, he quickly counted it. Sixty-odd dinars. About two hundred and fifty American dollars. George and the Bedouins watched him with glowing eyes. Kando glanced once more at the scrolls and shrugged his shoulders. Then he pushed them toward me across the desk.

"Much dirty paper for little clean paper," he said with a wry smile. "We hope it brings Your Grace happiness."

In a few minutes I was alone with the scrolls, but the emptiness of the money box was reproachful. I put it back into the desk drawer out of sight.

During the following days, I studied the scrolls minutely, often sitting before them simply as though I expected them to find mouths and relate their story. There was no question in my mind as to their antiquity, but had they been found in a desert cave? And what was the subject matter of their contents? I needed help in finding out. Otherwise, as Kando said, I had merely traded a little clean paper for much dirty paper.

I contacted George Shaya again and asked if he would check the cave's authenticity. He agreed to do so and after a few days reported that he had been with the Bedouins to the cave and had found many pieces of cloth wrapping on the floor and numerous broken jars. There was one complete jar as well, he said, and a piece of wood with a stone under it.

I listened avidly but could not help thinking that if between Kando and George there had been any collusion, George would of course back up their story with these added details. With this in mind, I prevailed upon him to visit the cave once more, this time in the company of Father Yusef, a quiet but astute and saintly man who had brought much credit to St. Mark's.

In August, they journeyed by bus to Jericho, then set out on foot toward Feshkha, to the storied cave. Inside, they found one jar that Father Yusef considered transport-

ing to our young monastery not far from there. He thought
it might be useful for cooling water during the summer
months. But its weight and the day's excessive heat discouraged him, and it was left there. Beyond that, he reported seeing only shreds and scraps of scrolls such as we
already had, and chips of wood and potsherds.

One thing was confirmed now. There *was* such a cave,
and it was in the vicinity of Jericho. All the old dreams
and conjectures swept back upon me. There was little else
I could concentrate on as the summer turned to fall.

Now for the contents!

I took into my confidence a member of my congregation,
one Stephen Hanna Stephen, who held a fairly important
post in the Department of Antiquities. He examined the
scrolls and listened politely to my stories of Origen and
the Catholicos Timothy.

"Your Grace," he said with a smile and a shake of his
head, "you have a romantic imagination. Bedouins are
forever *finding* ancient things in the desert and passing
them on to—you'll excuse me—to gullible buyers. If you
have not already done so, please take my humble advice
and don't pay one shilling for them. Return them whence
they came. They are worthless."

I tried to dissuade him but realized at the same time that
I had no real authority wherein to speak. To find words
to explain the intangible certitude that persisted within
me was impossible. Intuition is a precarious framework
for fact.

Mr. Stephen was graciously indulgent. "You may feel
that way, Your Grace," he told me, "but if I were you, I
should not voice such opinions too loudly. You do not
know, I think, how painful scorn can be."

"Scorn?" It was my first hint that such might follow a
serious effort to learn the truth.

"Certainly. If you should venture such opinions and be
proved wrong, you would not soon forget it. I have heard
of one such scholar so maligned that he took his own life in
despair."

In any case, I asked him, would he bring them to the Antiquities Department that the proper authorities might pass judgment upon them?

He looked at me with a mixture of amusement and pity. "Then I, too," he said, "would be involved, Your Grace — and probably thought a fool among my colleagues."

At least, then, would he ask an official to come to see me? He took up his hat and fingered its brim gingerly.

"I would prefer not to say a word to anyone, Your Grace. You would honor me not to insist."

Stephen left. Nervously, I paced my apartment floor. After all, I considered, his forte was as an Orientalist. Perhaps he knew no more than I when it came to Hebrew. There must be someone upon whom I could rely to offer a valid opinion. I thought of the excellent French Dominican school, École Biblique, and Father Marmadji. Fellow Syrians, he and I had had frequent and happy relations over the years. I went to see him and told him the story of the scrolls.

A few days later, he came by St. Mark's to inspect them, but though he found them curiously interesting, he could not share my feelings regarding their genuine antiquity. A week or so later, however, he returned with another Dominican scholar, Father J. Van der Ploeg, who wished to examine a book in our library in conjunction with studies he was then pursuing on the Eastern Churches. His work concluded in the library, I invited this learned guest into my quarters to view the scrolls. With great care, he examined them all closely.

"Your Excellency," he told me, "it would be next to impossible to find manuscripts as old as you presume these to be, but I believe the largest one is The Book of Isaiah. This small one also appears to be a work of the Old Testament, though I could not say which book on such short perusal."

The Book of Isaiah. One of the most popular of all Old Testament works — and the priest had recognized it immediately. Perhaps, after all, these were merely manuscripts from some recent or medieval genizah—a room near a synagogue where worn or damaged manuscripts are held in storage. Perhaps I should simply turn them over to the monastery librarian and forget all about them. I was sorely tempted. But an old, old dream is long in dying.

In September, official business of the archdiocese took me to Homs, in Syria, where the Patriarch maintained his offices. He was much moved by the discouraging reports of the agonies of war that were threatening in the Holy Land; and he talked at length of his deep concern for the many of our faith who faced an uncertain future.

Our conferences over, I related to the Patriarch my story of the scrolls and then produced them for his examination. His Holiness was well versed in history and science but he, too, felt that inexperience betrayed my judgment in regard to their age.

"We do not think that they can be more than three or four hundred years old, my son," he told me. "But then, we are not an authority in these matters, either. Take them to Beirut on your way back to Jerusalem. At the American University there you will find a professor of Hebrew who will surely enlighten you." His Holiness presented me with a letter of introduction before I departed. "And do not be afraid to make mistakes, Yeshue," he advised me. "A mistake can be the best teacher a man ever meets."

The professor of Hebrew was out of the country on his vacation, and the demands of the archbishopric would not permit me to await his return. By the end of September, I was back in Jerusalem knowing no more than I had known before.

Again I called on Stephen. "If I can convince no one else," I said to him, "I will at least convince myself."

"How do you mean, Your Excellency?"

"I will study Hebrew. Can you bring me some elementary books on the subject?"

"That is quite an undertaking, Your Grace. But if you are determined—"

I told him I was. He brought the books, and, as if some

of my certitude had at last communicated itself to him, he advised me that, against his better judgment, he was also bringing an "expert on Hebraica," a Mr. Tovia Wechsler.

Mr. Wechsler studied the scrolls peremptorily and confirmed Father Van der Ploeg's identification of The Book of Isaiah. "And where were these found again?" he asked tersely.

"By the Dead Sea. In a cave."

He laughed and swept his hand over the length of the table upon which the scrolls were lying. "Your Grace," he said, "if these came from the time of Christ as you imply, you couldn't begin to measure their value by filling a box the size of this table with pounds sterling."

Stephen smiled timidly at each of us, and they left the monastery. Gently, I put away the scrolls. Sooner or later, I believed, someone would vindicate my feelings about them.

A week or so afterward, a Dr. Maurice Brown called upon me. He was a Jewish physician interested in discussing a piece of property adjacent to St. Mark's, where there had been, until the last tenant's death, a much needed clinic.

Our real estate business concluded, I placed the scrolls before this highly educated gentleman and told him a little of their history. He said that he was unprepared to offer an opinion one way or another but suggested that I contact Dr. Judah Magnes at the Hebrew University. The rising tension kept me from acting on this suggestion at the moment, but he followed it through himself and a few weeks later two young men from the university's library called on me. They examined the scrolls carefully and discussed them at length in Hebrew. Then they advised me that they could not come to any conclusions on their own and would have to seek the advice of their superiors. Could they come again, they asked, and photograph a few columns for study? I assured them that they would be welcome to do so, provided the scrolls did not have to be removed from the monastery. With my hopes raised considerably, we shook hands all around and they left. They left, never to return.

Shortly afterward, the thoughtful Dr. Brown kindly sent another friend of his to see the scrolls. This man, Mr. Sassun, was an antiquity dealer of excellent repute and I welcomed his advice. His suggestion, however, was that I send pieces of the scrolls to friends of his in Europe and America for proper evaluation, but at a time when we were not certain that a postal card could go safely from one quarter of the city to another, I was reluctant to pursue such a course.

The autumn passed. Relations between Jew and Arab grew increasingly hostile, for the Arabs feared that the violence which so far had been directed largely at the British might be redirected at them.

On November 29, the United Nations General Assembly, meeting in their home in Flushing Meadows in the United States, recommended the partition of Palestine into an Arab state and a Jewish state, with Jerusalem and an area around it to be a separate demilitarized area under a UN mandate. The Arabs rejected this completely, and the word had hardly reached Jerusalem by radio when reckless, passionate rioting began to rumble through her narrow streets. Great Britain, historically the enforcer of law and order, had not voted on the partition and now obstinately announced that she would not implement the UN decision by her mandatory powers, nor would she permit a UN Commission to enter Palestine until just before the end of her official mandate nearly six months later. The entire Holy Land was thus thrown into political and criminal chaos.

During the ensuing days of strikes and killings, there was little time to worry about the scrolls, especially in the light of all I had heard to discourage me. Indeed, the only source that held out the mildest hope for the vindication of the scrolls was the Hebrew University, and the violent division of the city into Old and New Jerusalem now made any such contact all but impossible.

In January, however, I was approached by one Anton Kiraz, a parishioner of St. Mark's who had learned of the scrolls' existence. Since I had been able to assist him through some financial difficulties in the previous October, he offered his aid by way of returning a favor.

A few years back, he told me, ancient tombs had been discovered on a small piece of property which he owned, and at that time he had made the acquaintance of a genuine authority on matters of archaeology, Prof. Elazar L. Sukenik, of the Hebrew University. If I so desired, he would try to arrange a rendezvous with this gentleman at some safe place.

I agreed to let him try his hand. How ironic it would be, I thought, if at last I learned something definite about the scrolls through the mediation of a spasmodic church-goer who earned his living in the most modern of capacities — he taught people how to drive automobiles!

Somehow, Anton was successful. They met at the library of the Y.M.C.A. in Jerusalem which was situated in a security zone known as Zone B on Julian's Way. The librarian, Malak Tannourji, a member of St. Mark's congregation, permitted them to use his office and was a quiet witness to their transactions.

Anton removed the scrolls from a paper bag and showed them to the professor. He examined them intensely for a brief period and came to the conclusion that they could indeed be ancient. He asked permission to take them with him to the university for further study and also to permit Dr. Magnes to examine them. He promised to return them by the end of the week. Anton agreed. A few days later, the professor asked for an extension of two or three days. Again, Anton agreed.

On the appointed day, they met again at the Y.M.C.A. in the presence of Mr. Tannourji. The professor said that the university was interested in purchasing them and that he was certain that they were very old indeed. Anton agreed to negotiate with me and promised he would communicate with the professor shortly. On February 6, the

scrolls were back in my possession, and though the interest
of the university was revitalizing, it still did not answer my
questions: *What* were they? *Where* did they come from
originally? *How* did they come to be in a cave in the Dead
Sea wilderness? That a scholar was interested in purchasing them was good news indeed, but it was the secrets of
the scrolls themselves that fascinated me. I advised Anton
to inform me of any further word he would have from the
university, but I was not completely satisfied that this
should be their final disposition.

At about this time, Butros Sowmy returned to St. Mark's.
He had been on sabbatical leave in Lebanon for some
months, and with a joyful heart I welcomed my long-
standing friend and boyhood companion back to the monastery. Naturally, I confided in him all that had transpired
in his absence and, intrigued completely by the story of
the scrolls, he became the first human being to share my
enthusiasm fully regarding them.

At his suggestion, we telephoned Bishop Stewart at the
Anglican Cathedral and were given the names of Drs. William Brownlee and Millar Burrows at the American School
of Oriental Research. The latter, according to Bishop Stewart, was the Director of the American School, but was temporarily away at Baghdad. Without delay, Brother Sowmy
picked up the phone and called the American School.

I listened expectantly as he asked for Dr. Brownlee. A
search was made for him, but he could not be found. "Is
Dr. Burrows, the Director, there?" No, he was in Baghdad.
"Is there someone in charge at the moment?" Yes, a Dr.
Trever. "Might I speak with him . . . about some ancient
Hebrew manuscripts?" Just a moment.

"Dr. Trever," he said, "This is Butros Sowmy. I am a
monk at St. Mark's Monastery."

"St. Mark's," the cackle echoed.

"Yes. The Syrian Orthodox Monastery in the Armenian
Quarter."

"Oh, yes."

Butros raised his eyes to heaven, to seek understanding

if not pardon for what he was about to say. Then he took a
deep breath and proceeded: "We have been going through
the library here and we've chanced upon a number of manuscripts that are very old and appear to be written in Hebrew.
They aren't identified or listed anywhere in our catalogues,
and I was hoping one of your professors might throw some
light on them. I've had very pleasant relations with the
American School since the thirties and I thought perhaps
you might help me."

Silence for a moment from the other end of the wire;
coming into the Old City was not an easy matter at this time.

"Could you come *here*, Brother?"

Butros looked to me. I nodded quickly.

"Yes, Doctor. When would it be convenient?"

"Tomorrow. Is two thirty all right?"

"Fine, Doctor. Just fine. I'll be there."

"Good. I'll see you then."

"Yes. And thank you, Doctor. Thank you very much."

Smiling, Butros hung up the phone and addressed me
with the intimate but respectful title he had adopted since
my consecration as archbishop. "Sayidna," he said, "about
the cataloguing business — I thought it best not to get them
too stirred up."

I had to agree with him. I had already tasted the worm-
wood of sarcasm and incredulity.

The next afternoon accompanied by his brother, Abraham, who had now become a Customs Inspector on the
Lebanon border, Butros crossed over into the New City.
And with him went the scrolls, wrapped in newspaper,
carried in a small suitcase. (I keep it now as a souvenir at
my residence in Hackensack.)

I awaited his return with hope and anxiety. And this time
I was not disappointed!

Dr. Trever, he told me, had been greatly impressed. He
had examined the scrolls carefully, unrolled them as much
as possible without damaging them, and had even copied
some lines from them. "He was going to photograph them
as well," he added, "but his camera was at the museum."

"Did you tell him the truth about them?" I asked.

Butros grinned. "I had to, Sayidna. He seemed so sincerely fascinated with them that I could not resist revealing their curious history."

"And when shall we hear from him?"

"He said tomorrow," Butros answered. "But I shouldn't be surprised to find him here in the middle of the night."

Early the next morning, an intense, bespectacled young man presented himself at the monastery and introduced himself as John C. Trever. He was a Biblical scholar in his early thirties and a man of impressive accomplishments, not the least of which was his talent as a photographer.

He had identified the copied portion as the first verse of the sixty-fifth chapter of Isaiah, but more revelatory was the comparison of the copied lines with facsimiles of writings known to date from the early Christian centuries. And it was his unnerving belief that the scroll was of an even earlier date!

It was agreed that Butros and I would bring the scrolls back to the American School on the following day so that they might be photographed in detail. Then Dr. Trever asked to see the Isaiah Scroll once more. He unrolled it with infinite care, marveling as foot upon foot spread out along the library table, and he copied the beginning section of the very first column. This he would study to determine just how much of The Book of Isaiah the scroll contained.

As he finished his finely detailed copy, he yawned audibly. "Forgive me, Your Grace," he said with a shy smile, "I had difficulty sleeping last night. I could not take my mind away from the scrolls."

He did not have to explain his predicament. I knew exactly what he meant.

The following day, Saturday, February 21, Butros and I made our way through the Arab roadblocks into the New City. Closed shops and rubble-strewn streets offered bitter omens of the catastrophe that lay ahead for Jerusalem, but Dr. Trever had heartening news. The section he had copied proved to be the first chapter, first verse, of The Book of

Isaiah. It was now probable that this one scroll contained the entire work.

Despite terrorism, bombings, and machine gun fire which broke out sporadically in the streets of Jerusalem in those days, Dr. Trever (with the assistance of Dr. Brownlee) succeeded in photographing the Isaiah Scroll and the small buff-colored scroll on the very first day. They photographed also the exterior of the very black and brittle scroll which could not be opened. At the end of the day, Butros and I took these scrolls back with us to the monastery, leaving with Trever and Brownlee the two small white-colored scrolls which had not yet been photographed. On February 24, Drs. Trever and Brownlee, even more enthusiastic than before, returned the scrolls to the monastery. I welcomed them back as though they were prodigal children; but now, instead of there being two white scrolls, there was only one.

With a broad smile, Dr. Brownlee explained.

"No, Your Grace, we haven't lost any. On Sunday afternoon, Dr. Trever was studying them and noticed that the handwriting was identical and the parchment exactly the same size and color. Also, one ended with a seam and the other began with one—and they fitted together perfectly. He called me in and we fastened them together by splicing them with tape. Here, you see, between columns seven and eight. The break is hardly noticeable."

"Then I suppose its best to leave it that way," I remarked. Brother Butros winked at us, observing that "what the American School has joined together, no man should put asunder."

Dr. Brownlee deftly rerolled the two which were now one. "It is possible," he said soberly, "that these are among the oldest existing books in the world."

The next few days were spent processing the photographs. All of us waited breathlessly for whatever they would reveal.

On February 27, the photographs of the small buff-colored scroll were developed, and Dr. Brownlee was able to identify several quotations from The Book of

Habakkuk, followed by commentary. Habakkuk was an Old Testament prophet writing during the Chaldean oppression of the people of Judah. He it was who predicted, not long before 600 B.C., the ultimate deliverance of the Jews. He is most famous for his statement: "The just shall live by his faith."

Now two of the scrolls had been identified. In my Mass that Sunday morning, despite the tragic war engulfing us, my heart was bright with gratitude to Almighty God. Isaiah was there—complete, and possibly the most ancient account extant; the prophet who foretold most clearly the advent of the Virgin-born Messiah whose mission would induce the highest spirituality among both Jews and Gentiles. And now Habakkuk—who spoke with undaunted hope of a time when "the knowledge of the Lord's glory shall cover the earth as the water covers the sea." Both scrolls held vital messages for our troubled times. It was most fitting to recall Habakkuk's prayer:

O Lord, revive thy work in the midst of the years,
In the midst of the years, make it known.

Slowly it seemed that the scrolls were beginning to find the lips I had envisioned as I sat staring at them months before. Softly, as in a whisper, they were beginning to speak across the centuries.

On Monday, March 1, Dr. Trever and the Director of the American School, Dr. Millar Burrows, obtained passes from the Arab High Command and came to St. Mark's.

Dr. Trever had prepared a report for me on the work done thus far in which he explained that though much study and research would be necessary to determine a definite date or period of origin, they were undoubtedly ancient. There was no question, the report continued, but that in order to protect their great value to the study of the Bible and Biblical literature steps should be taken at once to insure their safety. It would be hazardous indeed, he observed, to leave them in Palestine at this time.

"And this one," I said, touching the shorter, blackened scroll.

"That scroll," Dr. Burrows explained, "will require experts to properly unroll it, considering the almost gelatinous state to which it has been reduced by the ages. See, even as we touch it, fragments sluff off here and there." On the tip of his finger he picked up a tiny piece. "Look!" he exclaimed suddenly. "*This* one isn't Hebrew. It's Aramaic."

Aramaic—the very language of Christ himself!

The political crisis expanded into a growing list of shootings, bombings, casualties, and death. Access between St. Mark's and the American School became more and more a matter of sheer courage.

Dr. Trever managed to rephotograph some of the Isaiah Scroll which had not come out to his expectations. Along with the other photos, he then presented me with a set of prints. Others he had dispatched by air to Dr. William F. Albright, an esteemed professor in the Antiquities Department of John Hopkins University in the United States.

On March 15, the professor replied ecstatically:

> My heartiest congratulations on the greatest manuscript discovery of modern times! There is no doubt in my mind that the script is more archaic than that of the Nash Papyrus. . . . I should prefer a date around 100 B.C.! . . . What an absolutely incredible find! And there can happily not be the slightest doubt in the world about the genuineness of the manuscript.

Upon learning of Dr. Albright's reaction, I retired immediately to the chapel to offer my thanks to the God who had seen fit to make steadfast my faith in the scrolls during the long months of neglect and disbelief. When I came from my prayers, Butros was waiting for me in my office.

"You've heard the news, Butros?" I asked him.

"Yes. I've just spoken to Dr. Trever. He thinks we should

store them in St. John's out near Ain Feshkha. From this moment on, we cannot take a chance of having them lost or damaged. Indeed, if a full-scale war erupts, St. Mark's will be right in the crossfire and, Sayidna, such a war is inevitable."

"I hope you are wrong, my brother," I told him. "But we must prepare for the worst. Do you think they will be safe in St. John's?"

"Not as safe as they would be in Beirut."

"Beirut?"

"Yes. In a bank vault."

He saw from my surprise that such a thought had never struck me.

"Do you remember," he continued, "what you told me the book dealer said last summer about pound notes filling the space of that table?"

I nodded. The man had indicated that so much money would not approximate their value—*if they had come from the time of Christ.*

Butros samiled. "That's just it, Sayidna. There's a strong possibility that they have. Shall I prepare for the journey?"

"You will leave in the morning."

On March 20, the gentlemen from the American School made arrangements to visit the cave in which the scrolls had been found. Dr. Trever had also obtained permission from Mr. R. W. Hamilton of the Palestine Department of Antiquities to examine the place and gather up any loose material he might uncover there. Their Bedouin guide, however, did not show up, and they were told that the trip was too dangerous in view of troop maneuvers being staged in that area by the Jewish Army.

In the next few weeks conditions grew almost unbearable. Transportation and communication services ceased to function. "It seems," Butros noted, "to be the beginning of the end."

There was little joy in the Easter of 1948. Attempts to obtain a truce had proved futile. Blood was demanding blood, and it seemed as though neither side would cease until the Holy City was a pile of smoldering rubble.

The American School was forced to close. Dr. Brownlee, who had prepared while still in Jerusalem the first translation of the Habakkuk Commentary, was the first to depart, leaving the last day of March. On April 2, Dr. Burrows followed, and at last, after a final conference and a heartfelt farewell, Dr. Trever left on April 5. The fires of our mutual enthusiasm had done much to weld our lives together in the past few months and to see them leave was, in the case of the younger Drs. Trever and Brownlee, to see my sons depart; with Dr. Burrows gone, a warm friend and adviser was absent from the scene.

But there was little time for sentiment in the terror-ridden weeks ahead. Nearly a quarter million Arabs were already homeless by the termination of the British mandate, and small Arab villages had been completely destroyed. There were Arab reprisals, but these were used as further reasons to expel them from their homes. In April, Zionists attacked the village of Dair Yaseen, slaughtering 250 peasants there, of whom more than half were women and children and thus, when the Arab armies entered Palestine after May 15, 1948, it was quite as much to protect the Arabs from Zionist atrocities as to prevent the fulfillment of the United Nations partition scheme. Hate bred hate and unreason spawned unreason until a time came when the onlooker could take no sensible side.

On May 14 shortly before midnight, the British calmly withdrew, glad to be relieved of all responsibility in the war-torn land. For months they had ceased to function as a responsible government, leaning over backward to act in strict neutrality; and now there would be no government at all without continued bloodshed.

The weekend that the British quit the land proved holocaustic; and St. Mark's precarious position between the Jewish and the Arab quarters of the Old City made it bear the brunt of shelling from both sides.

On May 15, Butros stood in the courtyard listening to the whizzing bullets, the bursting bombs. "Remember the ammunition that was stolen by the Tommies during the other war?" he asked me. I nodded. He cocked his head. "They couldn't find it then—well, there it is."

The next day an errant piece of it lodged in his skull and killed him instantly.

By mid-June, Count Folke Bernadotte, a gentleman and diplomat esteemed the world over, was appointed to head a peacemaking commission for Palestine. He attempted first to arrange for a cease-fire truce, but all proposals were rejected. On July 18, he tried again—this time with a little more success. Even Jews and Arabs were becoming tired of killing one another.

Through the spring and summer months, the scrolls lay secure in their Beirut vault. They had by this time been adquately identified through the photographic plates. There was the complete text of The Book of Isaiah in fifty-four columns of thirty lines each, beautifully written and neatly paragraphed. The Isaiah Scroll was made of seventeen sheets of carefully dressed leather and measured twenty-three feet, nine inches, in length, and ten and one fourth inches in height. The parchment was delicately ruled, and the letters were hung from the line, not written above it. As in other Semitic languages, the writing was from right to left. The second scroll identified was the Habakkuk Commentary. This document had thirteen columns constructed from two sheets of leather and would prove to be the most ancient Biblical commentary extant. The chief importance of the work was that it interpreted the prophecies of The Book of Habakkuk as having been fulfilled in the early days of the Jewish sect that owned the scrolls. Since the scroll did not quote the third and last chapter of the original prophetic book, it supported a view long held by many scholars that this last chapter was not originally part of the work but was an independent psalm, ascribed to Habakkuk, which was added at a later date. The Hebrew Old Testament was put into its final form in A.D. 90 at the Council of Jamnia. Therefore, a commentary upon a *two*-chapter edition of the book after that

The Aramaic Scroll of Genesis

date would not be conceivable.

The third scroll, which Dr. Burrows had named The Manual of Discipline was a non-Biblical work. It was constructed of five sheets of leather and contained eleven columns of writing, and it appeared to be complete. This scroll set forth the rites, beliefs, and rules of an ancient

One column from the Habakkuk Commentary

Jewish sect which was monastic in its ideals and organization. The order had apparently retired into the wilderness to prepare for the Messianic age predicted by Isaiah. The fourth, the matted scroll, still remained unopened.

Later I learned that other scrolls existed, scrolls which, had Father Gelph not turned away the Bedouins that morning, would also have come to St. Mark's.

As it turned out, they were purchased by Professor Sukenik and despite the hazards and deprivations of the war, he had made their investigation and transcription the chief work of his life. Those in his possession consisted of three scrolls: a second but fragmentary scroll of Isaiah, The War of the Sons of Light with the Sons of Darkness, and a lengthy hymn of praise known as the Thanksgiving Scroll. I first learned of these through a news release when, through journalistic error, the scrolls in my possession were noted as having been in St. Mark's library for twenty years. Professor Sukenik on reading this, rightfully sought to set the record straight and so announced his own purchase to the press. The Hebrew University, it must be added, had attempted a number of times to begin negotiations with me in regard to the other four, but since the American School had done so much to establish for me their identity and scholarly value, it seemed only proper to permit them the honor of first publication.

By now it seemed clear why the scrolls had been directed by Providence to St. Mark's. The monastery, its property, and school had been damaged during the shelling, and a thousand members of dislocated families throughout Jerusalem and Bethlehem were destitute, threatened with starvation and disease. The sale of the scrolls would do much to aid them.

I did not reckon, however, on the venality of men.

In August, a letter from America advised me: "Persistent rumors have been coming to us from another party . . . that you do not have title [to the scrolls] . . . entirely . . . but that another person has part title."

I racked my brain to think how such a rumor could have started, and who "another person" was supposed to be; but the pressing needs of the community and the congregation were such that I could not worry about rumors, "persistent" or not, when thousands of my people were dispersed in the surrounding countryside, forced to flee from calamity without furniture, funds, often without even clothing.

Early in September, another letter from America stated that in a published account of the discovery of the manuscripts as released through a Hebrew University-oriented publication, my *soi-disant* partner was none other than the driver-trainer, Anton Kiraz. The account went on to announce that preparations were being made to publish facsimiles from *both* the Isaiah Scrolls!

Needless to say, I was astonished. The photos taken by Dr. Trever had never left St. Mark's. How could they then be published? Then I realized that back in the early winter, still not knowing what the scrolls contained, I had permitted Anton Kiraz to arrange a showing to Professor Sukenik. They had remained in his possession ten days. Time enough for anything.

Still, happier news came in the same mail. A final agreement had been reached between the American School and myself by which they would have exclusive publication rights for three years. In the light of the implied complications, this was a reassuring stroke of luck, for I was advised from every side that though I could not anticipate a great deal of profit from such a scholarly venture, the publication and distribution of the scroll material could not help vastly increasing the demands for the originals and subsequently, of course, their value on the market.

September took me to the Patriarch in Homs to report on the urgent relief needs of our people, and I told him of the numerous refugees who had come to the Old City of Jerusalem. The situation was even more dire than His Holiness had imagined.

"We shall have to ask much of you in the days ahead," he told me quietly. "There is a great deal of work to be done, Yeshue, if we are going to make our Christianity a living reality for our people." Humbly, I told him I was prepared to do whatever he and my fellow bishops deemed necessary.

On September 17, Count Bernadotte was assassinated by Zionist terrorists. The fires of warfare flared again, and again, as usual, the innocent suffered most.

On October 19, His Holiness sent a letter to the faithful in America, imploring them to do all in their power to assist their countrymen in the ravaged Holy Land. In order to facilitate this campaign he honored me singularly by appointing me Apostolic Delegate to the United States and Canada.

My mission would be to collect relief, consecrate churches, and ordain new priests. Through each of our official church bodies in the New World he urged their cooperation with me and encouraged them to do their utmost to assist St. Mark's and the Jerusalem refugees. This appointment could not have come at a more auspicious time, for I had just received word from America advising that the only possibility of selling the scrolls there would be to make them available in that country for the inspection of prospective buyers.

A longshoremen's strike just after Christmas delayed my sailing for a few days, during which time I stayed at the Hotel St. George in Beirut often in the genial company of Dr. Bayard Dodge, who was also awaiting the *Excalibur*'s departure.

The word "saintly" would not be ill-used to describe the learned but humble Dr. Dodge. Having read a great deal about the scrolls, he was intensely interested in hearing all that I could add to their fascinating history. We looked forward to sailing together, though at one point I assured him that if the strike did not end soon, I would probably have to go by plane instead.

"Strike or no strike," he cautioned me, "don't you go by plane. Stick to the boat, Your Excellency." When I asked why he had said this, his candid reply made me smile but also gave me substantial food for thought. "You are carrying with you a treasure, Your Grace — a valuable legacy to knowledge. The good earth has preserved these scrolls for thousands of years — if the plane should catch fire or crash, the whole world would feel the loss."

A few days later the *Excalibur* weighed anchor, and I was aboard her with the scrolls that the cave of Ain Feshkha

had laid at my feet. My hopes were high. My faith in their
genuineness could not again be ignored or berated. Even
my melancholy at leaving my beloved land behind me
could not depress me. After all, I would return soon, bringing relief, and, I prayed, honor to my people. The shores
of Lebanon sank below the horizon. Soon only the wooded
crest of Mt. Sannin could still be seen and in a moment
that too was gone from sight.

Alexandria, Piraeus, Naples, Genoa, Rome—it seemed
that all the cities of history came and went as we traversed
the Mediterranean. Then the great stone of Gibraltar

*First day of the author's arrival in the U.S.A. Procession
through the streets to the Church of the Virgin Mary in
West New York, N.J.*
Photo by George Sanders Photo Service

loomed beside us and there was only ocean, mile after mile of ocean, and at its end, the New Land, the sturdy youngster of history, the country Father Dolabani had once called the "hope of the world"—and now my hope and the hope of my people as well. Like a sailor signed up with Columbus, I strained my sight daily for the first glimpse of that fabled shore, and when at last the towers of Boston rose like a gray graph against the skies, the tears in my eyes were not entirely the result of the wind or the salt sea spume.

When the *Excalibur* docked in Jersey City, New Jersey, an impressive throng of priests and laymen were on hand to welcome me. The delegation was led by Father Elias Sugar, pastor of our church in West New York, N.J. We left immediately for the church, and the ceremonies there began with a procession through the streets that reminded me strongly of occasions in India years ago when I had toured with the late and beloved Patriarch Elias III.

The West New York Church, consecrated by our Patriarch Ephrem I during his visit as Apostolic Delegate, had been built in 1927, and while ascending the steps in the full regalia of office, I caught sight of the title over the door. In Syriac and English there was inscribed: Assyrian Apostolic Church of the Virgin Mary. It seemed a novel appellation to me, and referring to a national people whom history had decreed lost since the seventh century B.C., curiously contradicting. But then, this was America—great, beautiful, powerful America, a nation of individuals—and it *all* seemed like a dream.

On Sunday morning, I officiated at a Solemn Pontifical Mass assisted by Father Sugar, Father Peter Barsoum, Father Poulos Samuel, and Father Stephen Dorghali.

Following the Mass, I looked out over the crowded church and prepared to deliver my first address in America. It was touching to see their expectant and sympathetic faces turned toward me. Here, thousands of miles from the lands of their origin, they had found a new world. Most of the older members, I was told, were employed in their ancient crafts of sewing and carpet-making. But there were many bright faces of the young also—the children who had risen to responsible positions in myriad businesses and industries. How could I tell these healthy, contented people of their brothers?

How could I delineate for them a precise picture of deprivation and destruction? How could I create for them the reality of hunger, despair, and naked fear? The poorest of the congregation before me had arrived in automobiles that their Near Eastern brethren could never dream of owning. Could I, in an adopted tongue, recreate for them the tragedy of the Holy Land? I prayed for Isaiah's burning coal to touch my lips as well, and then the faces, the prosperity, the contentment before me, blurred. I saw my friend and fellow monk Butros sprawled on the courtyard stones, his life ebbing away in a ribbon of scarlet flowing from his temple. I saw those wild eyes that would wink no more, that crooked grin forever vanished. I blessed the congregation and began my sermon.

During the next few months, the parishioners maintained me in rooms at the Hotel Plaza in Jersey City while we set about the task of establishing a responsible relief committee to deal with our widely scattered branches throughout the United States and Canada. And I also found time to reestablish relationships with my friends from the American School of Oriental Research, whose activities in their homeland centered around Yale University.

Work on the publication of the scrolls progressed rapidly, and hardly a day passed without some new voice rising from the scholastic or archaeological circles proclaiming their wonder to the world. We learned from Jerusalem that investigations of the cave at Ain Feshkha by Father Roland de Vaux and G. Lancaster Harding had produced evidence dating from the second century before Christ, and hopes rose high that the University at New Haven would be able to purchase the scrolls and thus guarantee these priceless documents a safe, permanent home in a free and peaceful nation.

But on February 25, there was mailed to every prospective buyer a shocking statement. It was a notice, printed in simple style and bearing only a New York City street number as a return address. It stated that the scrolls in my possession had been removed illegally from the country and appealed further to "all persons and bodies" to refrain from purchasing them.

Despite the fact that learned scholars and gentlemen of unquestioned integrity stood by my personal claim of ownership, this document, and the subsequent rumors it stirred up, did irreparable damage.

Among these scholars and gentlemen was Dr. W. F. Albright, whose word had first confirmed the original views of Drs. Trever and Brownlee. I had the pleasure of meeting with him personally in March, and after due consideration, he advised me that the estimated value—if indeed such things could be assigned a monetary equivalent—could not be less than $180,000. Since the Isaiah Scroll was complete and at least a thousand years older than the next oldest Hebrew Biblical scroll now known, he ventured the opinion that for that scroll alone, a hundred thousand dollars was an absolute minimum "below which no intelligent man versed in books would dare to go."

Early in April of 1949, it was my privileged duty to consecrate a new church, St. Ephrem's, in Central Falls, R.I. In an age-old ceremony, I ascended a small stepladder at the east wall of the church and anointed the wall with holy oil. This was repeated at each wall of the building while the clergy, deacons, and archdeacons chanted the office of consecration. (Later on, I assigned Father A. Doumato to serve this only Syriac-speaking parish in the United States.)

But my joy that day was tarnished. Only hours before a letter had reached me which said that claims were being made demanding the return of the scrolls by the governments of both Israel and Jordan—governments that had not even existed at the time of the discovery of the scrolls!

These reports were distressing, but I could not allow them to interfere with either my mission here in America or my obligations to the world of scholarship. Later that week I entrusted to Dr. Trever a matted mass of fragments that George Shaya had also reportedly found in the cave. He examined them carefully and separated them, layer by layer of dry, brittle leather, which he removed and photographed, finding evidence of three separate scrolls that had jelled together through the centuries. Portions of the fragments seemed to come from The Book of Daniel, the remaining sections from an apocryphal Hebrew work.

Through the late spring, I stayed near the New England activity, at our church in Worcester, Massachusetts, and made the fortunate acquaintance of one Charles Manoog, a Syrian-American who was to prove confidant, friend, and brother to me very often in the difficult days ahead.

During that time, I received a letter from none other than my erstwhile parishioner, Anton Kiraz. Naturally, he said not a word about the scrolls or his contentions regarding them but he did inform me that he had been stricken with tuberculosis and was hospitalized in Beirut. My cordial feelings for this fellow had been much diminished, of course, by the trouble he had brewed with the Hebrew University by representing himself as a partner in the ownership of the scrolls; but since he was apparently not pursuing that nonsense and since by his letter I presumed that he did not know I had learned of his activities, I took his plea at face value and sent him a hundred dollars that I had recently realized from Dr. Trever's sale of photographs.

Early in June, I was advised that Yale University could no longer consider purchasing the scrolls. They had recently raised a great deal of money to buy original material by the English diarist Boswell and could not expect to realize another such transaction in the near future. This was the offered explanation, but a few days later I was given even clearer proof that other considerations had influenced their decision.

Since late winter the problem of unrolling the fourth scroll had been paramount in the minds of all scholars and interested parties; and the urgent needs of my community were sufficient to make me consider the possibility of selling the scroll unopened. Advisers nevertheless assured me that having it opened would considerably increase its value, and so steps in this direction had been taken.

The problem was placed with the authorities of the Fogg Museum of Art, of Harvard University. In their letter of June 7 outlining the estimated costs, time elements, etc., that would be involved in the unrolling project, they made it clear that one of their conditions would have to be a clarification of ownership.

"We should want to be certain," they wrote, "that the Israeli Government has no claim on it."

So once again this senseless ghost had risen to haunt me. If anyone other than myself had any claim to make against my possession of the scrolls, it would have to be the British Mandate Government of Palestine—a government inept and indifferent through its last years of authority, and a government that now no longer existed. Israel did not have at that time, and had never acquired, control over the area in which the scrolls were found. Their claim was absurd.

As for the British Mandate, among the first persons to view the scrolls had been Stephen Hanna Stephen from their Department of Antiquities. If there had been a claim by them, surely he would have so advised me. Hoping for his clear opinion in the matter, I prepared a letter seeking his advice. I never mailed it. The following day I learned that Stephen was dead.

And the Near East was not the only direction from which clouds of confusion were sullying the horizon.

The connection was bad but the voice needed no identification. The precisely modulated tones instantly announced my friend and adviser from Maryland.

"Your Grace," he said to me after an exchange of pleasantries. "It is your business surely, but I'm wondering if an auction block is the proper place for a sale of the scrolls.

After all, they are imbued with the dignity of scholarship as well as the dignity of your position in the church and I—"

I interrupted him. "I'm sorry—I don't quite understand what you mean."

"The scrolls—I've just read that they are to be put to auction in Baltimore later this year."

"Auction? Baltimore? Wherever did you read that?"

"The newspaper—*The Baltimore Sun*—didn't you—"

"I certainly did not. There are plans for an exhibition of the scrolls in Baltimore in November, but I could not consider auctioning them, and no one was authorized to say so."

"You will have to watch that, Your Grace. A false story such as this could deter many parties who might otherwise be interested."

"Yes. I understand."

"And I suppose the price also is exaggerated somewhat?"

"The price?"

"Yes. It says further on in the story that you are asking a million dollars."

I held the telephone a moment in stunned silence. Would there be no end to misconceptions and false reports?

As soon as I could reach him, I asked Dr. W. F. Albright to act as a press clearing agent for me in that area. He graciously agreed to do so, insisting as always that he would accept no honorarium for the service. He was above politics and partisan camps. His genuine interest was in advancing scholarship and that alone. His services proved inestimable to me.

But, of course, that original story had already been circulated. The barn, in effect, was locked now; but a dangerous horse was running loose.

My episcopal duties took me now to Detroit, Michigan, where our people there had kept ties with their ancient faith through a Society of St. John Chrysostom until the Patriarch was able to provide them with a pastor. Working together then with Father Stephen Dorghali, they had at last raised up their own parish church of St. John Chrysostom. In August of 1949, the honor of consecrating it fell to me.

From there, I journeyed to Canada, where fifteen hundred adherents still lacked both priest and parish, and from there to Jacksonville, Florida, where an equally large congregation was forced to hold services in the Homs Brotherhood Hall.

Certainly there was much to be done if our Syrian Church in America was to reflect the splendor of our long and glorious history. She needed priests, she needed churches, and equally important, she needed those seemingly minor things to create the proper atmosphere and tradition by which a heritage is safely passed from generation to generation. I spent much of the time preparing Syriac prayer books and language-teaching guides for the younger members of our congregations, and everywhere I traveled I was met with enthusiasm and faith in the future. Community councils were being formed across the length and breadth of this land, and there was even talk of interceding with the Patriarch in hopes of creating an activated archdiocese here in the United States.

Back in New England, reasonably assuaged by my published statement that I was willing to expound my claims to personal possession of the scrolls to any certified court of law in the world, the Fogg Museum proceeded cautiously.

They had not yet touched the unrolled scroll which was thought by this time to contain the apocryphal book of Lamech, but they had mounted the others and covered them with a protective plastic case. As for the unrolling, it was estimated that time and work costs would amount to $2,000. The American School of Oriental Research was able to offer one half of this as chargeable against final publishing costs, but even so, I had no way to raise the additional thousand dollars. Also, the museum, quite sensibly, wanted the scroll insured against loss or damage while it was in the unrolling process, and the insurance premiums, which they also felt I should personally provide, were quite beyond my means, for the insurance would have to be upwards of $50,000!

During the summer, the Hebrew University and the American School had come to an agreement effecting the mutual exchange of photographs between the scholars of both camps. The agreement—which was restricted to scholarly work on the documents and had been entered into with my express consent—did not specifically deny the former claims of the Hebrew University as to the ownership of the scrolls, but at the same time it did not imply or give any basis for such claims, and I fervently prayed that *that* controversy had been laid to rest.

The newspaper story from Baltimore, however, had raised new difficulties. A friend arriving from the Holy Land in September had heard that the Arab tribe was threatening St. Mark's Monastery with an astronomical lawsuit, claiming that they had been paid a pittance for documents said to be worth millions of pounds sterling! Thus had one local wild report exploded into the internationally fantastic. Undoubtedly, the scrolls had come to be incredible ammunition in the war of nerve and propaganda that continued to divide my homeland.

"Until the tension has eased," my friend advised me, "you would be wise not to return to Jerusalem."

Not to return to Jerusalem! I could hardly believe at the time just what was happening. I had purchased the scrolls on the strength of a story that seemed to leap from the pages of science fiction. I had paid for them with every penny I personally possessed. I had believed in them and had found rejection at every turn in the road, and I had relinquished my dream of keeping them in St. Mark's only because the people of my community were in such desperate need.

And suddenly, I was a thorn in the side, indeed, almost an enemy, of all I cherished most dearly in the world. Not to return to Jerusalem. . . . He might have told me not to breathe again the scents of morning, not to pray, not to smile, not to sing. What should I do?

Now, to injury, inevitably was added insult. The Government of Jordan (ignoring the facts that the scrolls had been found, purchased, *and* removed from Jerusalem prior to its existence in Jerusalem) publicly declared me a smuggler!

And all of these things conspired to prevent the only final hope I still held out for the scrolls—their sale to an American institution. Even the gala premiere at the Library of Congress did little to raise my spirits as the summer of 1949 faded into autumn.

The Library of Congress, working in conjunction with Dr. Carl Kraeling of the American School, spared no effort to make the exhibition of the scrolls there an excitingly memorable occasion, but much credit must also be given to a unique and genuinely humble human being named Lester Plowman who, perhaps among all people I had met or would meet in connection with the scrolls, seemed most truly representative of the miracle that is America.

By profession Lester Plowman was a boilermaker. He earned his living in the steaming shops of the Baltimore and Ohio Railroad. Somewhere along the way, as happens often with young men everywhere, Lester had lost his faith, but a chance attendance one night at a suburban Baltimore church impressed him, and since the lecture-meeting dealt with Biblical archeology, it stirred within him a sense of history and an intellectual curiosity to find out about the past. This led him first to Dr. Albright at Johns Hopkins, thence to the study of archaeology, and at last back to his early Christianity. Having left school at sixteen to become an apprentice boilermaker, the limitations of his formal education presented serious drawbacks to his professional pursuit of this scholarly subject, but he persevered and trained himself. During World War II, while building barracks and airfields in Hawaii and the Philippines, he pursued his studies in every spare moment and began gathering books that have since expanded into an impressive library. At last, specializing in

the religious aspects of ancient daily life, he prepared a
manuscript dealing with the relation of history to the Old
and New Testaments and while checking a point and seeking advice from Dr. Albright, the story of the scrolls came
to his attention. As soon as possible he made a trip to see
me in New Jersey; then he contacted scholars at Yale and
at last solicited the interest of the Library of Congress
and the Walters Art Gallery in Baltimore. Many a learned
and highly paid official would share in the success of
these exhibits, but the seed that blossomed forth so re-
wardingly for them was planted first by a railroad boilermaker—who in the loneliness of his modest rooms had

Mr. Lester Plowman and the author

trained himself for a task he could not foresee.

During the exhibition at the Library of Congress, the scrolls were guarded twenty-four hours a day by those same men who preserved the safety of the Declaration of Independence and the Constitution of the United States. On Saturday evening, October 22, the exhibition was offi-

The exhibition at the Library of Congress, 1949. In the middle: the author; and on his right, Dr. Luther Evans, Director of the Library of Congress, surrounded by the congregation who came with the author
Photo by the Library of Congress

cially opened by Dr. Albright, who addressed the assembled dignitaries on the great antiquity and importance of the scrolls and on the unique place they would
forever hold in Biblical literature.

Then the Director of the Library, Dr. Luther H. Evans,
led us to the glass encasements, where I drew back the
cover from the scrolls. The Isaiah Scroll was opened to
the second chapter, and the fourth verse, an appropriate
admonition ringing across the centuries:

> *They shall beat their swords into plowshares,*
> *And their spears into pruning hooks;*
> *Nation shall not lift up sword against nation,*
> *Neither shall they learn war any more.*

During the next two weeks, well over fifteen thousand
people would read and consider these forceful and inspiring words. November 10–17, 1949, a similar success was
realized at the Walters Art Gallery, of Baltimore, and a few
days later I received encouraging word from Dr. Evans,
who contemplated the possibility that the scrolls might
someday return to the Library of Congress for permanent
custody. Needless to say, this had become my cherished
hope as well.

Early in November the introductory material for the
first volume arrived for my study and approval. My only
objection was that the introduction did not state the probable date of the scrolls' origin. But it was explained to me
that having the material photographically at hand, scholars
would be free to come to their own unbiased opinions regarding the antiquity of the scrolls. I was disappointed,
since I had hoped an authorized published statement on
their dates would facilitate the matter of selling them, but
the publishers had their valid reasons and I deferred to
them.

As the publication date drew nearer, interest and enthusiasm in regard to the scrolls mounted considerably.
Dr. Kraeling began conferring with a nonsectarian Protes-

tant library for the study of the Bible and the Christian Church i.e., the Christian Zion Research Library, which, upon learning of the financial difficulties surrounding the opening of the fourth scroll, offered, in exchange for an exhibit of that scroll, to provide the additional thousand dollars.

This, along with a thousand dollars provided by the American Philosophical Society, was all that we needed, except for the urgent matter of insurance, and, at last, on January 6, the Fogg Museum agreed to underwrite the

Exhibition of the Aramaic Scroll at the Christian Zion Research Library. From left: Dr. Carl H. Kraeling; Miss A. Marguerite Smith; the author; the Very Rev. Peter Barsoum; and Mrs. Mary B. Frederwick, President of Zion Research Foundation
Photo courtesy of The Christian Science Monitor

premiums. It seemed now that nothing stood in our way.

The Christian Zion Research Library is housed in the wing of a Victorian sandstone castle. It is a beautiful and imposing structure with a uniquely romantic history. The home, originally constructed in the State of Michigan, had been transported brick by brick over twelve hundred miles to Seaver Street in Brookline suburban Boston, where it was rebuilt to the very last nail. Its tapestried, satin-lined walls create rooms of soft splendor — a fit setting for this most enigmatic of the scrolls.

"It seems such a shame, doesn't it, Archbishop?"

I presumed that this well-dressed woman referred to the fact that the scroll had yet to be unrolled. I nodded and smiled, as if to say "it will be taken care of soon."

"I suppose we should count our blessings that we had them with us for a while. I understand they are all beginning to crumble to dust."

I was for an instant startled into silence. "I beg your pardon?"

"Perhaps I'm an eavesdropper, Archbishop — it's an old New England custom — but before you arrived this afternoon I heard some of the gentlemen talking. I gathered from what they said that the rest of your scrolls have all but deteriorated. From exposure to the air, I would imagine."

Later that evening, I repeated this incredible observation to the late Miss A. Marguerite Smith, a gentle authoritative woman who was then in charge of the library's precious collection.

"Yes, Your Grace," she told me. "I've heard some similar comments. Of course, I refuted them whenever I did encounter them, but apparently it's a very widespread rumor."

And despite the original preservative measures applied by the Fogg Museum staff and considerable improvements rendered to the scrolls by the experts at the Library of Congress, this rumor was being noised about in precisely those circles from which I had hoped a final purchaser would appear! It was a frustrating development.

I thanked Miss Smith for her kindness. In the days ahead, that refined and genuinely Christian woman would warrant my gratitude time and again. She was an indispensable source of friendship and encouragement—and these elements would be sorely needed.

A letter from the Jordanian Department of Antiquities carried other disconcerting news a few weeks later.

There will not be any question now, it read, *disputing your ownership* of the scrolls. This was to say the least a welcomed concession, but the text continued with the notice that since there was still a belief that the scrolls had been removed illegally, it would be necessary for me to return to Jordan with the scrolls and obtain the necessary governmental releases.

Whether or not this was a ruse to bring the now famous documents back to that country did not matter. If there was no question "disputing my ownership," there should also have been no question concerning my right to have removed the scrolls, and the demand for me to return to Jordan to satisfy the red-tape measures of a department that had insinuated its rulings retroactively upon me was altogether invalid.

The vacillatory attitude of the Fogg Museum added further difficulties. Still obsessed with old tales of multiple ownership and fearing that substantial damage could possibly occur in the unrolling of the fourth scroll, they now demanded that I post a bond large enough to encompass the total estimated value of the document.

Mr. Charles Manoog, the son of one of the very first Syrians to arrive in this country, had worked diligently for years to build up a successful and reputable plumbing concern in Massachusetts. To him, the scrolls were a source of great pride in his people and his church, and he had all but supported me since my arrival here, but I could not permit him to involve his livelihood and his business in such a risky endeavor.

"No, Charles," I told him. "You and a few others have

done so much more than your share already. For the museum even to suggest this, knowing that I depend on members of my congregations from one meal to the next, is cruelly ridiculous. I have offered them goodwill, cooperation, and sincerity. That was all I had to offer. It seems it was not enough."

Except for the brief visit with the people of the Christian Zion Library, the only bright spot in my life during that winter came with the exhibition at Duke University in Durham, North Carolina. This was held February 12–17, 1950. My visit there was especially joyful because I was able to spend some time with the esteemed Dr. William Brownlee, who was then Instructor of Religion at Duke. His presence had inspired the university to undertake the display. The actual arrangements were worked out by a very gracious man, Rev. George Ehlhardt, who was the Divinity School librarian there. Dr. Brownlee, who had been the first to identify the Habakkuk Commentary, was at that time preparing the first translation of The Manual of Discipline. He delivered a lecture at a banquet for a North Carolina librarians association in which he argued persuasively for both the antiquity of the scrolls and for the kinship of the sect with the Essenes. This thrilled me very much. He also did his best to encourage Duke University to purchase the scrolls, but to no avail. The problem there, as also in many universities, was preoccupation with a building program calling for millions of dollars to meet the needs of postwar expansion.

In addition, the widely distributed publications of the American School facsimiles actually had served to decrease somewhat the desirability of purchase — if scholars and institutions the world over had ready access to readable photographs, what need did they have of the originals?

Throughout these days of doubt and discouragement, a chief source of comfort and strength came from the advice and companionship of George B. Kedersha, a member of the New Jersey Bar and my good friend and counselor at law. He gave much of his valuable time and knowledge of legal complexities for the safety and promotion of the scrolls.

In the spring, with a leaden heart, I reluctantly brought the still unopened fourth scroll back to New Jersey and placed it again among its renowned brothers. I could not permit the continued controversies to usurp my life. My duties were primarily to God and to his church. If the scrolls were not serviceable to the needs of my people, we would simply wait until they were.

During the remainder of 1950, clergy and laity from all our congregations worked arduously with me to raise relief for our brethren overseas. By October, St. Mark's Monastery and the Jerusalem Diocese, the Patriarchate in Homs and refugees in Lebanon and Jordan, and schools in Bethlehem and Amman saw the fruits of our coordinated efforts, for, from our small and scattered churches in the United States came contributions totaling nearly $15,000 plus uncounted packages of clothing. Knowing the work and sacrifice which had gone into this campaign, the reality of Christian love and generosity was a vital inspiration for me.

In November, through the good offices again of Dr. Carl Kraeling, another exhibition was scheduled at the University of Chicago and shortly before I was to deliver the scrolls, a most distinguished visitor asked permission to inspect them.

Eugene Cardinal Tisserant, Dean of the College of Cardinals and Secretary of the Vatican's Congregation for the Church in the East, was himself an esteemed authority in matters of antiquity and during his days as head of the Vatican Library had discovered a Syriac manuscript on Isaiah dating from the fifth century A.D. The staff of the New Jersey Trust Company to whose vaults the scrolls had been temporarily entrusted, had hitherto paid scant attention to the documents; but a visit from so celebrated a churchman apparently impressed them, and Mr. Paul Bestar, the bank's manager, and his assistant, Mr. Arthur Miller, outdid themselves in welcoming the Cardinal and making his audience relaxed and comfortable.

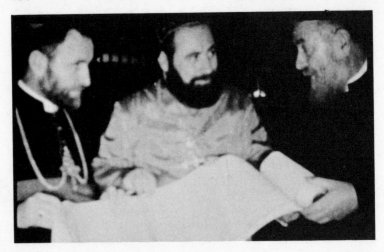

*Examining the Isaiah Scroll in the vaults of the Jersey City
Trust Company. Left: Archbishop Jarjour of Beirut, Leb-
anon; center: the author; right: Eugene Cardinal Tisserant,
Secretary of the Sacred Congregation for the Oriental
Churches*

Cardinal Tisserant apologized for the absence of Francis
Cardinal Spellman, of New York, who had been prevented
by diocesan duties from accompanying him as planned.
Then he proceeded to examine the scrolls minutely. Indeed, he assured me, these were considerably older than
his own Syriac discovery. I amiably suggested that perhaps
these, too, might someday grace the renowned Vatican
Library in Rome. He smiled and replied, *"In-sha-Allah,"*
which means in English, "If God wills."

And that afternoon as we walked together from the bank
out into the harsher glare of the early winter sun, it struck
me that no matter how much trouble and discord they had
caused, the scrolls had also done much, much good, for
here on this New Jersey city street, and in the museums and
study halls of Israel and Jordan, they were bringing together in concert men from many divergent creeds, men

from myriad walks of life. Indeed, Isaiah again had aptly phrased it: *The wolf shall also dwell with the lamb, and the leopard shall lie down with the kid; and the calf and the young lion shall fatten together.*

On Nov. 16, 1950, I left New Jersey accompanied by Mr. and Mrs. Charles Manoog to exhibit the scrolls at the University of Chicago. The exhibition at the University of Chicago was, from a prestige point of view, overwhelmingly successful. It was held November 17–26, 1950. Dinners and cocktail parties in the very highest social circles throughout that Midwestern metropolis preceded the opening ceremonies, and the atmosphere was redolent with wealth and the American counterpart of aristocracy. At that time also, coincidentally in Chicago, another test was being applied to determine the date of the actual origin of the scrolls — and this test was totally indifferent to history, religion, archaeology, or scholarship.

Dr. Willard F. Libby, of the university's Institute for Nuclear Studies, submitted samples of linen wrappings from the Ain Feshkha cave to what has come to be known as the "carbon 14 test." On January 9, he reported to Dr. Kraeling that this revolutionary way of measuring the carbon 14 elements that enter all living things had determined beyond a reasonable doubt that the linen had been flax one thousand nine hundred and seventeen years before, with a possible margin of two hundred years on either side. That meant that plus or minus two hundred years, these wrappings and the scrolls which they had held existed in the year A.D. 33!

This was the most encouraging news of all. Surely now that paleography, archaeology *and* nuclear physics had combined to support the many scholars avowing their antiquity the scrolls would be vindicated for all time, and some individual or institution would recognize the importance of providing a permanent home for such a treasure. But despite the overwhelming evidence of their antiquity, another bubble was ballooning into a bomb.

In 1929, Mr. Phinehas of Jerusalem, a Jewish bookseller

The exhibition of the four Dead Sea Scrolls at the University of Chicago, 1950. In the center stands the author, and to the right, Dr. Carl H. Kraeling
Photo by David L. Taylor

and a close friend of our late Bishop there, had presented a Torah to St. Mark's as a token of his interest in our library. As none of us there read Hebrew—an oversight in our seminary's curriculum for which we have paid dearly—we knew only that the Torah represented a good man's act of friendship. Other than the fact that it was an Old Testament scroll in Hebrew, there was little we could determine regarding it, least of all the date of its inscription.

Now at the time of the first interest exhibited by the fellows of the American School, they had visited our monastery and our library on a number of occasions and, of course, had had the opportunity of examining the many beautiful books housed therein. During one such visit they had examined this Torah, and were assured that although in Hebrew, it was not from the collection of scrolls found near the Dead Sea. It had not been necessary to so advise them, for to their trained eyes every mark of lateness was immediately apparent.

Some months before, accompanied by Mr. Stephen Hanna Stephen, Mr. Tovia Wechsler had also examined the scrolls and some other books from our library, and although he had not conceded their value at *that* time, now that the manuscripts and the conjectures surrounding them had become the foremost topics of the international scholastic world, he, too, decided to assert himself.

Claiming that he had been the first to identify the Isaiah Scroll, he maintained that he had been misled about their antiquity because he had also been shown a Haftarot Scroll that was obviously medieval. A Haftarot, or collection of readings from the Old Testament, is used in synagogues on solemn occasions and is a familiar work to any educated and religious Jewish male. Mr. Wechsler undoubtedly fell into both categories, but his contention that such a scroll existed in St. Mark's Library was entirely unfounded. Still, it served in many circles to fan the flames of cynicism that seem to surround any earthshaking discovery. As the poet has told us: "All looks yellow to the jaundic'd eye."

Drs. Burrows and Trever brilliantly remonstrated against this new accusation in many learned publications, principally suggesting that Mr. Wechsler had been mistaken in his hasty perusal of the documents either by the aforementioned Torah or else by quick conclusions based on his inspection of the Isaiah Scroll or The Manual of Discipline. For my part, I immediately wrote to Father Gelph at St. Mark's, authorizing him to permit the examination of any Hebraic scrolls extant in the library there.

The matter seemed settled for the moment, but this new contention and the suspicions it raised regarding a suppressed document found a curious support in the simple act by which Drs. Trever and Brownlee had so many months before pieced together the scrolls that now formed The Manual of Discipline. The circulation of stories that *five* scrolls had originally existed where now there were known to be only four added considerable fuel to the fires of suspicion and distrust.

In April of 1951, my three-year agreement with the American School ended. The scrolls were still unsold, still draining my small resources by their continued upkeep and the time and money necessary to defend them from their enemies, and I had realized only the sum of three hundred dollars from their published facsimiles.

Needless to say, my joy at their original discovery had been severely tested. As if there were not already sufficient odds against the possibility of their ultimate sale, that summer Dr. Solomon Zeitlin, the eminent editor of the scientific publication *The Jewish Quarterly Review*, announced that he was quite sure that the scrolls could date from no later than the Middle Ages. He utilized the Wechsler assertions to further surmise that Arabs had stolen these scrolls during their pillage of the Jewish section of Hebron in 1929 and had conspired with antiquity dealers to stage their discovery and thus enhance their monetary value. The scrolls, he concluded, had little value for either Biblical scholars, historians, linguists, or students of religion.

Hebrew University professors and authorities at the

American School were equally stunned by this new detraction, and again the pages of daily newspapers and erudite publications became the lettered fields of furious battle.

In order to conserve funds, I had at the invitation of my trusted friend Charles Manoog removed the scrolls to a specially constructed storage space in his home, and in October he arranged a very successful exhibition at the Worcester, Massachusetts Museum of Art. A few weeks later, Marguerite Smith provided for another showing at Vassar College. My heart was sickened with the name-calling and the controversy, however, and it was with something akin to relief that I at last replaced the scrolls in their vault and left for Canada, where a happier task awaited me — breaking the ground for our very first Syrian Orthodox Church in that nation.

By this time, it had become all but impossible to keep abreast of the stories appearing about the scrolls. News weeklies, Sunday supplements, religious magazines, and scientific publications bombarded the reading public with report after report and theory upon theory. It was as though a writer had only to attach the words "Dead Sea Scrolls" to his title to insure an article certain publication. Tear-sheets, clippings, commentaries, reached me from the most unexpected corners of the world of printed communication. For example, *Popular Science,* an American magazine on mechanics and handicrafts, in its December, 1951, number, issued a report on the carbon 14 tests of Dr. Libby, so that there among companion pieces such as "The World's Fastest Scooter," "How to Carve a Pipe," and "What to Do If Your Floors Are Sagging" was again the story of the scrolls under the title "Atomic Clock Verifies Oldest Bible Manuscript." A friend noted on the back of the copy he mailed to me:"It seems as if everyone and his brother are profiting from the scrolls except the man who owns them."

But the ways of God, inscrutable though they are, are nonetheless wondrous, for the scrolls had introduced me to a land and a new branch of my people, and had given me hope that our ancient church might truly find its proper place someday in this great nation, and *that* at least (and in the final picture, infinitely more important) seemed to be coming to pass. On May 13, 1952, His Holiness issued a decree appointing me Patriarchal Vicar to the United States and Canada, with the understanding that if during the next two years our people in those lands demonstrated their desire, capacity, and ability to maintain a centralized archbishopric, their churches would be established as a diocese and I would become their spiritual leader in the sister nations. The honor thus bestowed upon myself and the congregations throughout this continent was humbling in its scope, but it left us also strongly challenged to prove ourselves worthy of the tribute.

A zealous congregation proved equal to the task, and on November 15, 1957, in the first year of His Patriarchate, His Holiness Mar Ignatius Jacob III, Patriarch of the Apostolic See of Antioch and of all the East, set his seal upon the document proclaiming myself Archbishop for all our churches in the United States and Canada.

By the end of August, St. Ephrem's, our first church in Canada, was ready for consecration, and I knew then that the people would fulfill their part. I prayed that Almighty God would continue me in grace and health that I might fulfill mine.

Father Elias Sugar, who had visited this zealous but unfortunately priestless congregation as often as possible over the years, had been much of the force behind the construction of the beautiful new house of God. Now I had arranged for a French-speaking priest, Father A. Carim Karma, from Homs, to be installed as their pastor, and Father Sugar's emotion during the opening ceremonies was visibly moving.

"This church," he told the assemblage, "is the result of fond hopes kindled many years ago. My work with you is finished. When I come back again, it will be as a friend and a visitor, for you will soon have your own pastor, your

Consecration of St. Ephrem's Church at Sherbrooke, Quebec, 1952
Photo by Gerry Lemay

own priest. I urge you, I know you will, welcome him with open arms."

Brightly dressed women in the congregation touched dainty handkerchiefs to the corners of their eyes; and sturdy, robust men twitched their noses and restrained their feelings. For each beginning must by nature mark the end of something. They loved their Father Sugar. They would grow to love their new priest equally. And if a peasant boy from the fields and hills of Mesopotamia could come to be the spiritual leader of such noble, sincere Christians, of such zealous, hardworking priests, was anything at all in this great world impossible?

Upon my return to America, I resolved that the scrolls could no longer rob me of time and energy. Through the good office of Charles Manoog, a trust fund was estab-

lished to incorporate the scrolls and to provide for specific
charitable purposes in the event of their final sale. In February of 1953, I was advised that "enemies of the scrolls"
were still "making trouble," but I was determined to allow
the trustee to handle all matters pertaining to the documents. The archbishopric and my church properly became the most important aspects of my life; and if on Saturday, April 11, 1953, the *New York World-Telegram and
Sun* was willing to give considerable coverage to the
"slashing onslaughts" of Dr. Zeitlin, who was now publicly
proclaiming that "the Bedouin story smells" and declar-
ing the entire proceedings "a hoax," I could no longer
worry about such attacks.

More important to me was another story in the *Detroit
News* of that same date announcing the fact that at High
Mass on Sunday I would confer upon Father Stephen
Dorghali of St. John's the highest honor permissable in our
canons for a married priest. That he should be called "Very
Reverend" now was infinitely more meaningful to me than
the *Telegram*'s statement that a Dr. Harry Orlinski, of
Hebrew Union College, had joined Dr. Zeitlin's camp of
suspicion and had referred to the Dead Sea Scrolls as
"St. Mark's garbage."

But history has a way of catching up with her detractors.
Among the continued incredible finds centering around
the cave at Ain Feshkha was the excavation of nearly an
entire monastery dating from the last centuries before
Christ. Coins, letters, fragments, pottery, even furniture
hewn from stone, were wrenched from the covetous barrens of the Dead Sea desert. *The New York Times* of July
26, 1953, announced the discovery of a reconstructed text
of Euripides by an expedition sponsored by Louvain University—a text purporting to date from years before Christ!

Later in 1953 the people of our churches obtained a permanent residence for their new Archbishop, a comfortably
dignified brick home, with graceful colonial front columns,
and situated on a quiet residential street. Hackensack, New
Jersey, because of its centralized position among our

widely scattered parishes, proved an ideal headquarters from which to dispense the duties of my office. For a while of course, it would be necessary to hold divine services in the study or living room. But this was only the first step of an enthusiastic people; talk was already in the air regarding a proper cathedral. A small number of devoted and faithful families met with me in 1958 to discuss the question of purchasing a site for the erection of a cathedral. Soon afterward, I learned about the availability of a church situated on the corner of Fairmount and Grand Avenues in Hackensack. The purchase was consummated, and they all applied themselves with wholehearted vigor to the task of repairing and decorating the edifice as a cathedral, which we named St. Mark's after the monastery in Jerusalem. It is with great pride that I mention this episode in acknowledgment of the immense sacrifices made by those few families.

I would, of course, have to relinquish my title as Archbishop of Jerusalem; but as I wrote to my mother (promising to send for her in the event the appointment became official), "as the youngest church official in our hierarchy, perhaps my place is here with our youngest diocese. I will miss our people in the Holy Land, as I will surely miss the daily inspiration derived from moving along the streets and stones once hallowed by the presence of Our Lord. Since that day so long ago when we first reached the city, Jerusalem has been my home and yours, and all that I humanly love resides there. But my work, my life, now is bound up with this brave, this bright America and its headlong rush to a dazzling future. There is much to be done if our church is to share properly in that tomorrow. . . . But often, nonetheless, I will, with the prophet, mourn *if I forget thee, O Jerusalem.*"

As for the scrolls, they had abided through two millennia, awaiting the day when God would desire them to be revealed. I had learned patience from them in the face of adversity. I, too, could abide.

The call came early in May of 1954. It was long distance —

Montreal. I could not guess who the caller could be.

"Good afternoon, Your Excellency," my friend said as he identified himself. "Have you seen the papers?"

Busy with correspondence that morning and planning an immediate trip to the Jacksonville congregation, I had only glanced at them. I told him this slowly, taking the moment to prepare myself for whatever new charges, suspicions, villifications, I might now learn of.

"A school here—McGill University—has just purchased some of the Dead Sea Scrolls."

"Has—what?" It seemed impossible. Certainly, Israel would not sell hers, and if the story referred to the scrolls now held in trust, it was a brazen fabrication.

"No, Your Excellency," he explained. "Not *the* Scrolls. As a matter of fact, it was only a group of fragments. They purchased them from the Jordan Government."

"Did they reveal the price paid?" I asked.

"Yes, Your Excellency. Fifteen thousand dollars."

Fifteen thousand dollars—for *only a group of fragments!*

Certainly the time was ripe now for a more direct approach. I had considered advertising, but the trustee, Mr. Charles Manoog, did not encourage me. I paced the floor of my study. Is this the time? I asked myself. Is this the way?

Dear God, help me to know the right course, I prayed.

In the *Wall Street Journal*, page 14, June 1, 1954, in a one and a half inch space between "Summer Homes Available" and an "Established Manufacturer" seeking sales representation, there appeared the announcement:

Miscellaneous For Sale

THE FOUR DEAD SEA SCROLLS

Biblical manuscripts dating back to at least 200 B.C. are for sale. This would be an ideal gift to an educational or religious institution by an individual or group.

BOX F 206. *Wall Street Journal.*

And so it was done.

Among the replies arriving the next day was one that the trustee considered especially promising. It was from a Director of the Chemical Bank and Trust Company of New York and inquired after further specifics. Mr. Charles Manoog, who at my insistence had arranged for the advertisement, dispatched a description and a history of the scrolls, and advised that we would be happy to encourage negotiations, provided the bank's client already had some knowledge of their historic value and material worth.

An appointment was made for the bank official and Mr. Manoog to meet in New York City a few days later, and discussions were amiably begun. After lengthy negotiation, a price of $250,000 was agreed upon. If the client accepted this figure, Mr. Manoog promised to contact me in Jacksonville and conclude the exchange. My duties to the Florida parishioners were paramount now. If the scrolls had waited for two thousand years in a dry, dusty cave, they could well wait out another week or so in a cool, immaculate vault.

On July 1, I returned to New York. With Mr. Manoog, who had transported the scrolls with him in his car from Worcester, Massachusetts, and our attorney, Mr. Abodeely, we met Mr. Sidney Esteridge, the purchaser, and his lawyers in rooms at the Waldorf-Astoria.

Final wording of the contract and its supplements took us well into the afternoon, and an "expert," identifying himself only as Mr. Green, accompanied by several Hebrew scholars, arrived to verify the authenticity of the scrolls that we were offering.

As the weighty legalities progressed, my eyes were drawn again and again to the transparent perspex boxes that separately preserved the Scroll of Isaiah, the Habakkuk Commentary and The Manual of Discipline, and to the small wooden box, padded with cotton, wherein the supposed Lamech Scroll still held its secret council. Within hours they would pass from me forever. What curious destiny permeated all that they touched! For myself they

had once been a source of indescribable joy and the fulfillment of a lifelong dream; but they had become the center of stormy controversy, of rancor, suspicion, even hate.
Now perhaps with this American and his plans for them,
they would find their long-deserved place of honor, a peaceful sanctuary where they could continue to light the way
into the darkness of antiquity.

I walked to the window and looked out over the dizzying spectacle of soaring, sun-struck skyscrapers and down
upon hundreds of scurrying New Yorkers. It seemed most
meet and just that the scrolls should find at last a home in
this great nation and create at the same time the where-
withal to aid and educate the less fortunate in the ancient
lands of their origin.

By the following morning, the Dead Sea Scrolls were
the legal property of Mr. Esteridge. As it is written: *The
Lord giveth, and the Lord taketh away.*

On October 7, 1952, a charitable trust known as the
"Archbishop Samuel Trust" was formed in Massachusetts,
and the check for $250,000 was turned over to the trust at
this time.

A deep peace descended upon me, calling to mind the
tranquil holy hours spent in the Monastery of St. Matthew
high in the mountains of Mosul. Among the first bequests
of the Trust Fund was the subsidation of new constructions
at that ancient, ageless abbey and the addition of several
new rooms to the Monastery of St. Gabriel in Tour-Abdeen.

In February of 1955, I was startled to read in the morning
papers that Moshe Sharett, the Israeli Prime Minister, had
announced in the Knesset, or Parliament, of his country
the acquisition by Israel of the four Dead Sea Scrolls
"which had fallen into the hands of foreigners—to wit,
an Arab churchman."

Three years later, Yigael Yadin, a retired general and a
noted archaeologist, the son of Professor Sukenik, who
had first acquired the other scrolls, published a book. It
was entitled *The Message of the Scrolls.* In it, he candidly
outlined how, fearing that international tensions or personal

animosity might have prevented the purchase had he openly conceded that the scrolls were going to Israel, he had acted cautiously behind the scenes of the exchange.

He had happened to be, coincidentally, in New York City for a lecture at the time of the *Wall Street Journal* announcement and though he had not seen it himself, it was brought to his attention by an alert reporter named Monty Jacobs. Acting immediately, he had contacted his government in Israel and friends in the business world of New York, and his plan went into action. From years of underground activity with the Haganah, he had become an expert in subterfuge and strategies and, despite his notable war record, this campaign may well be remembered as the most distinguished of his career.

Ironically, his book also revealed that Mr. Green, upon whom the State of Israel relied for a final confirmation, was none other than Prof. Harry Orlinski, who had earlier called the precious scrolls "St. Mark's garbage."

The years go by. Housed in their own beautiful new building, fittingly called "The Shrine of the Book," the scrolls have rejoined those others separated from them one morning by the slam of a door. Historians, scholars, theologians, and scientists continue to fill libraries with the knowledge derived from them. Men of all faiths and nations meet and debate and confer; erratic writers who had once hoped to challenge the uniqueness of the Christ through these documents have withered before the overwhelming evidence that no tenet of Christianity need stand in fear of revocation.

The lion of human history is lying down with the lamb of our spiritual heritage, and the Little Child continues to lead us onward. The scrolls are beacons in the night of vanished centuries. May they burn brightly forever along the road to Truth!

I end. But God's praise continues.

If there be a portion remaining, it remaineth to thy knowledge, O Creator of the Worlds, and if there be a portion remaining, the Lord be the guardian thereof and to me pardoner and absolver.

—Prayer from the Liturgy of St. James, said as the priest cleanses the sacred paten

NOTES ON UNPUBLISHED FRAGMENTS

The obverse and the reverse of a fragment of the scrolls from the Qumran cave are shown below. Fragments were folded and stuck together like fig leaves.

Obverse

Reverse

These I kept till I could ask Dr. Trever, a student at the American School for Oriental Research, to open them. He found that they were composed of seven small pieces, two of which were in "square" Aramaic, from The Book of Daniel. The first was part of two consecutive pages showing Daniel 1:15:16 and 2:3-6.

The second contains a page in two parts, from Daniel. Here is the first (Daniel 3:24-30).

In both these passages the text does not differ from the traditional text, except in minor details.

Here are other pieces successfully pieced together by Dr. Trever without any clues to go on, by simply matching what appeared to be contiguous words, etc. It is not to be taken as exact, but at least it is obvious that we have to do with liturgical prayers such as are used by the Syrian Orthodox Church, in which occur similar expressions. Or they might be from a commentary on one of the books of the Old Testament, or even poetry written in continuous lines, with the plural sign giving the rhyme. This appears in most of the lines:

Among these tatters there were small pieces containing only one, two, or three letters, which might be useful in completing passages from Daniel or those of some other book. They are smeared with something like pitch, to which scraps of the linen wrapping are clinging. I understand the Bedouins have burned a lot of them, which were in a rotted condition. Here they are pieced together:

It will be observed that the texture is coarse, like that
of the burlap now in common use in the Middle East.

Along with these, there were small pieces of parchment,
on which were crude writing, undecipherable because
many of the letters were destroyed by wear or by insects.

Finally, pieces of papyrus were found, inscribed in
"square" Aramaic, similar to the Nash Papyrus in the
British Museum. They are completely undecipherable.